CW00456420

Bert van Dam

Artificial Intelligence

23 projects to bring your microcontroller to life!

Artificial Intelligence

23 projects to bring your microcontroller to life!

Bert van Dam

Elektor International Media BV
Postbus 11
6114 ZG Susteren
The Netherlands

All rights reserved. No part of this book may be reproduced in any material form, including photocopying, or storing in any medium by electronic means and whether or not transiently or incidentally to some other use of this publication, without the written permission of the copyright holder except in accordance with the provisions of the Copyright, Designs and Patents Act 1988 or under the terms of a licence issued by the Copyright Licensing Agency Ltd, 90 Tottenham Court Road, London, England W1P 9HE. Applications for the copyright holder's written permission to reproduce any part of this publication should be addressed to the publishers.

The publishers have used their best efforts in ensuring the correctness of the information contained in this book. They do not assume, and hereby disclaim, any liability to any party for any loss or damage caused by errors or omissions in this book, whether such errors or omissions result from negligence, accident or any other cause.

British Library Cataloguing in Publication Data
A catalogue record for this book is available from the British Library

ISBN 978-0-905705-77-4

Prepress production: Autronic, Blaricum
First published in the United Kingdom 2009
Printed in the Netherlands by Wilco, Amersfoort
© Elektor International Media BV 2009, second print March 2012

079029-1/UK

Content

Introduction

Man had always assumed that he was more intelligent than dolphins because he had achieved so much...the wheel, New York, wars, and so on, whilst all the dolphins had ever done was muck about in the water having a good time. But conversely the dolphins believed themselves to be more intelligent than man for precisely the same reasons[1].

Douglas Adams, The Hitchhikers Guide to the Galaxy

In 1995 an article by Watanabe[2] was cause for commotion. It appears he had trained pigeons to distinguish the difference between paintings by Picasso and Monet, a feat previously assumed to be impossible. The pigeons received a reward if they pecked a switch, but only if a painting by Picasso was shown at the same time. Initially the pigeons pecked completely at random. After a while however they stopped pecking if a Monet painting was shown, and only pecked if a Picasso was shown.

In the tutorial project a yellow and green LED are switched on at random by a microcontroller. The microcontroller can be "rewarded" for its choice of color by pressing a button. If that happens the microcontroller will be more inclined to select that particular color. Eventually the microcontroller will learn that you like this color best, and therefor limit itself to picking just this one color.

The program learns in the same way the pigeons did in the research. Does that mean the program is artificially intelligent? The behavior of the program and the pigeon is identical, so from that point of view one might answer this question with "yes". Pigeon brains however work totally different than our program, so from that point of view the answer might be "no". Nobody knows how pigeon brains work, and the question is: does it matter?

Because this is a book on microcontrollers and computers, and not on philosophy we will take the position that a program that behaves intelligent is in fact intelligent. The difference in inner workings between the brain and the software will be regarded as the difference between biological and artificial intelligence.

---

[1] Douglas Adams, The Hitchhikers Guide to the Galaxy, published Del Rey (1995), ISBN-10: 0345391802.
[2] Watanabe, S., Sakamoto, J., & Wakita, M.: "Pigeon's discrimination of paintings by Monet and Picasso", Journal of the Experimental Analysis of Behavior 63 (1995), pp. 165-174

In this book we attempt to build learning machines and artificial intelligence with programs that are as simple as possible. The advantage is that the behavior can relatively easily be understood. At the same time the results are most astonishing: sometimes very little is needed for intelligent behavior.

The programming language used in this book is JAL[3]. All sources and supporting software can be downloaded from the website www.boekinfo.tk, so you can get started straight away. A bit of knowledge on electronics and electronic parts is recommended. If you want to know more about the JAL programming language, microcontrollers or how to build microcontroller electronics the book "PIC Microcontrollers"[4] is highly recommended.

This book is loaded with footnotes referring to scientific articles, books or websites. It is not a requirement to actually read these articles: all information you need for the projects that are described is contained in this book. The footnotes are meant to help you find additional information on the fascinating world of artificial intelligence[5].

I would like to thank Joep Suijs and Stef Mientki for their help in editing the Dutch version of this book, and Kyle York for his help with the English translation.

Bert van Dam
Roosendaal, 2008

---

[3] Just Another Language, a Pascal-like high level language. It is the only high level free language and has a large international user group. JAL is freely configurable by use of libraries and can be combined with assembler.

[4] PIC Microcontrollers, 50 projects for beginners and experts by Bert van Dam. This book covers 50 fun and exciting projects such as a silent alarm, people sensor, radar, night buzzer, clock, vu-meter, RGB fader, serial network, poetry box.

[5] A convenient way to locate scientific articles is by using the Google Science search engine http://scholar.google.nl/

1 Your most favorite color (tutorial)

A program that will learn which color you like best: yellow or green, and humor you by predominantly switching that LED on for you.

Software

This tutorial is meant to test your hardware and the correct installation of the software, but at the same time it will result in the first learning program. In fact this is a simplified version of the roulette wheel brain which is discussed in more detail in chapter 4.

In this project a microcontroller randomly switches a yellow or green LED on. This is done by casting a die. If the result is smaller than a threshold (called *choice*) than the yellow LED will be switched on, if the result is equal to or larger than the threshold the green LED will be switched on. Even if you have no knowledge of JAL the language is easy to read:

```
-- roll the dice
select = dice

-- compare with the threshold value
if select < choice then
    yellowled = high
else
    greenled = high
end if
```

You can "reward" the microcontroller for its action by pressing a button. The result of this reward is that the chance of selecting this color LED is increased.

```
if switch then
    -- reward received, encourage the current behavior
    if (yellowled) & (choice <= 6) then choice = choice + 1 end if
    if (greenled) & (choice > 0) then choice = choice -1 end if

    -- wait for the user to release the switch
    while switch loop
        delay_10ms(1)
    end loop

end if
```

If you press the button while the yellow LED is on the value of *choice* is increased by one. This means that in this part of the program

> if select < choice then
>   yellowled = high

the chance that the yellow LED is switched on has increased. Of course it would be useless to increase the value of *choice* above six because this is the highest value a die can cast.

For the green LED the same applies because *choice* is reduced when you press the button. It is important that *choice* is never smaller than zero. Since *choice* is defined as a byte this would mean it would suddenly be large again, because $0 - 1 = 255$.

The result of repeated adaptations of *choice* is that the microcontroller learns that you like this color best, and for that reason only switches on this particular LED.

Hardware

The hardware is simple and consists of a 16F877 with a switch and two LEDs[6]. The schematic and the picture of the breadboard can be used to build this project.

You are advised to mount a small 0.1 uF capacitor on the four corners of the breadboard to prevent power irregularities. You need to use a proper stabilized power supply, preferably with a UA7805[7] power stabilizer chip, see section 12.4. These remarks apply to all projects. If you use the Wips648 programmer a power supply is already built in.

---

[6] You can also use the 16F887A. In that case you need to change the include file from 16f877_bert to 16f877A_bert in every source.
[7] The UA7805 can supply 1.5 amps max, but then you need to use a decent size heat sink. For the projects in this book a heat sink of approximately 6 cm^2 is enough. Make sure the supply power to the UA7805 has a sufficiently high voltage (9 to 24 volts).

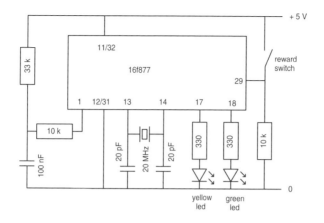

Figure 1. Schematic of the tutorial project.

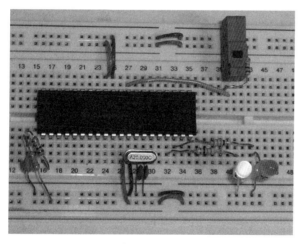

Figure 2. Tutorial project on a breadboard.

Because this is a tutorial project you will receive some additional technical information such as the pin layout of the 16F877 microcontroller. In the next section you will find instructions on how to program this microcontroller.

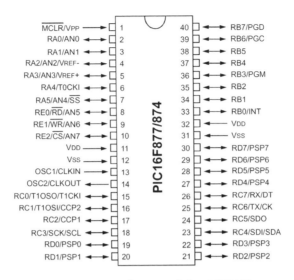

Figure 3. Pin layout of the 16F877

Instructions

On the website www.boekinfo.tk you can download the free software package that comes with this book. Install the software according to the instructions in the website. Then start the JALedit[8] program

Using *File.. Open...* you can load the tutorial software called *tutorial.jal*. The source is color coded for easier reading. You can check the code for errors by compiling it. Click on the button with the green triangle on it.

A window will open and shortly afterwards in the "compile results" section at the lower part of the screen the compiler results are shown. These will start with:

jal 2.3 (compiled Jun 23 2007)
0 errors, 0 warnings[9]

---

[8] You can also use your own editor. In that case you need to follow the instructions that came with that editor, and perhaps you miss some features that are discussed in this book such as color coded syntax, one button compile and download, library and function overview etc.

[9] If you use another JAL version you will find another number and another "compiled" date.

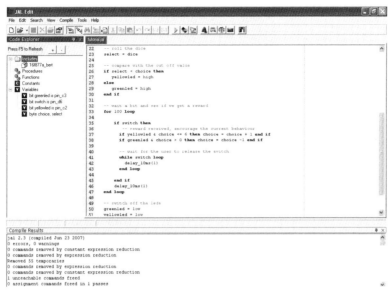

Figure 4. JALedit with the tutorial program.

Following these two lines are many others, but they're not important at this point. No errors, by the way, doesn't mean your program will do what you want, or even work. It simply means you haven't made any syntax errors. Let's assume, for example, that you accidentally entered *ouput* instead of *output* you would immediately get an error message like this:

jal 2.3 (compiled Jun 23 2007)
[Error] (tutorial.jal) [Line 9] "ouput" not defined
1 errors, 0 warnings

The compiler reports that the error has been made on line 9.

Connect the programmer Wisp[10] as indicated in the following table. In all projects with the 16F877 microcontroller the programmer needs to be connected in this same manner.

---

[10] This book assumes that you use the recommended programmer Wisp (628 or newer). If you use another programmer you need to change the settings of JALedit accordingly. (*Compile.. Environment... Programmer*) and follow the instructions of your programmer. The Wisp is an in-circuit programmer. If your programmer isn't then the microcontroller must be removed from the project (with the power switched off) to allow programming, make sure to follow the instructions that came with your programmer.

Color	Connection
yellow	pin 1
blue	pin 40
green	pin 39
white	pin 36
red	+5 volt
black	ground (0)

Switch on the power and on the PC click on the button with the integrated circuit and the green arrow (compile + program), or press Ctrl-F9. The active[11] JAL file will now be compiled and sent to the programmer. The compile window appears again, but this time it is followed by a window with a black background. This second window belongs to the software of your programmer, in this case the Xwisp2 software.

Figure 5. Download window.

You can observe the progress of the download in the black window. After downloading the program to the microcontroller the program is automatically checked to confirm that downloading was successful. If everything is OK one of the LEDs will be switched on. You can reward the program for this color by pressing the button. If you don't like the color

---

[11] The active JAL file has a blue tab. Please note that even if you are working in another tab the blue one will be compiled.

simply don't press the button. After a while the 16F877 learns which color you like best and will only switch on that LED.

Every project has a section called "optional". Here you will find suggestions to change the project, or expand it. Some suggestions are rather simple, others may require you to study for a while to find a solution. In the latter case a hint is sometimes provided. These suggestions are meant to stimulate you to see the projects in this book not as a finished project, but as a starting point for a lot of experimentation fun. This tutorial project also comes with a suggestion, this time with a small hint.

Optional

Once the program has learned your taste you can't change it anymore, because the other color will not be shown again. Try to adapt this program in such a way that changing your preference is possible.

Hint: You can use a second button to "punish" the program for showing a color that you don't like. Once you have these buttons you can check for yourself why inconsistent rewards and punishments never lead to the desired behavior, for example by sometimes rewarding and punishing for showing the exact same color. This doesn't just apply to "educating" microcontrollers; it also applies to educating children .

Debugging

If everything went well you can skip this section and go straight to chapter 2. If it didn't go as planned look for your symptom in the table below and follow the instructions.

Symptom	Remedy
The window with the black background doesn't come up.	1. There are errors in the program. Check the window at the bottom (compile results) for error messages. 2. You didn't install the downloaded software package correctly. Some software is missing or cannot be found, particularly the programmer software (xwisp2). Carefully read the instructions of the download package and follow them exactly. 3. You have installed the software to a different location than instructed. Go to "environment options" in the "compile" menu, select the "programmer" tab and enter the correct location. Note that <u>spaces are not permitted</u> in directory or file names.

Symptom	Remedy
	4. You have connected the programmer to a comport other than port 1. Go to "environment options" in the "compile" menu, select the "programmer" tab and add port x to the line that contains "go", where x is the comport number that you are using. So if you use com 4 this line would become "port 4 go %F". Note the space between port and 4.
The window with the black background shows a lot of complicated text and then disappears.	1. The programmer is not connected or not connected correctly. Switch off the power and connect the programmer correctly (all wires!). 2. The power is off. Switch it on and retry. If you use a breadboard make sure the top and bottom power rails (and segmented rails) are connected. 3. Another program is using the same serial port as the programmer, possibly a terminal program. Close the program and try again. You may need to restart the PC if the program doesn't release the port. 4. Your power supply isn't stabile enough. Make sure you use a stabilized power supply where the voltage is maintained at the proper level with, for example, a UA7805. Make sure the voltage of the transformer used to feed the power supply is high enough. (See section 12.4 for the requirements.) Do not forget the 0.1 uF capacitors on the four corners of the breadboard. 5. The voltage of the power supply is not 5 V. Even though you can sometimes program at 4.7 V, this usually doesn't work.
The program is downloaded but the LEDs don't come on.	1. The LEDs are connected backwards. Insert them in the opposite direction. 2. The LEDs are connected to the incorrect pins. Switch off the power and check all connections.

The program and the hardware schematic contain no errors. If despite the instructions above the program still won't work check everything again and again. Perhaps it's best to call it a day and check again tomorrow. Sometimes a good night's sleep does wonders.

If you're still convinced that you've done everything right then meet us in the JAL usergroup at Yahoo (see http://www.boekinfo.tk for the correct address and post your question). Note that this is an international group with users all over the world, so the mandatory language is English.

2 Games

In this chapter we will discuss two games in which the microcontroller uses artificial intelligence in an attempt to beat you. The first game, paper-scissors-rock, uses psychology. After you have read the story you won't fall for it of course (or will you?). Try the program on someone who hasn't read the book and be amazed.

The second game, Nim, learns from its mistakes in much the same way you would. Not by using game theory or smart tricks, but simply by remembering what didn't work out, and by not doing that again. After a while you are guaranteed to loose from this program, even if you do know the game theory.

2.1   Paper-scissors-rock

The rules for paper-scissors-rock are very simple. Both players count simultaneously out loud from one to three and then show a symbol with one hand. A level flat hand represents paper, a fist represents rock and two fingers in a vertical V represent scissors. The scissors beats paper (because a scissors can cut paper), the paper beats the rock (because paper can be wrapped around the rock) and the rock beats the scissors (because the rock will dull the scissors). If both players chose the same symbol the game ends in a draw.

Paper-scissors-rock is a game of balance. The three possibilities are in balance with each other. In nature this situation occurs very often, for example in bacteria that are involved in the production of antibiotics.[12].

But it also occurs in a lizard family, the Uta Stansburiana. The males of this species have an orange, blue or yellow throat, and each kind has its own mating strategy[13].

- Orange throat males are the strongest, and rarely engage in monogamous relationships. They fight over females with the blue throat males. So orange beats blue.
- Blue throat males engage in monogamous relationships. They are stronger than the yellow throat males. So blue beats yellow.
- Yellow throat males are the weakest, but they look a bit like females. Due to their disguise they can mate with females that really belong to the orange throat males

---

[12] Kerr, Benjamin en Bohannan, Brendan, Stanford University, Nature, 2002 Jul 11;418(6894):171-4

[13] Sinervo, Barry & Zamudio, K. R. (2001): The Evolution of Alternative Reproductive Strategies: Fitness Differential, Heritability, and Genetic Correlation Between the Sexes. *Journal of Heredity* 92(2): 198-205

(particularly when they are engaged in fighting) but not those who belong to the blue throat males for they are monogamous. So yellow beats orange.

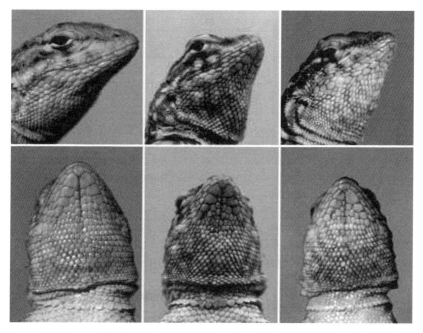

Figure 6. Orange (left), blue (middle) and yellow (right) throats of the Uta Stansburiana lizard[14].

So it boils down to orange beats blue, blue beats yellow and yellow beats orange. The number of lizards for a particular throat color remains stable in the long run, but is subject to serious fluctuations in the short run. Over a period of 4 to 5 years a particular strategy (and thus throat color) is dominant. Then it will decline because the strategy that can beat it is gaining strength. This process repeats indefinitely.

Paper-scissors-rock is a pure game of chance; there is no winning strategy, as the lizards show, assuming that all players make random moves. The table shows the average score for each possible move. You get two points when you win, one point in a draw and no points when you loose. If your move is paper than your average score over a large number of games will be one.

---

[14] Picture Barry Sinervo van de University of California, Santa Cruz. A color version of this picure can be found at the support website www.boekinfo.tk

		opponent's move			my score
		paper	rock	scissors	(average)
your move	paper	1	2	0	3/3 =1
	rock	0	1	2	1
	scissors	2	0	1	1

People are experts in pattern recognition, and for that reason they will rarely make random moves, because even in our own behavior we recognize patterns. If you ask someone to name three random numbers smaller than ten, you will virtually never get four-four-four as answer. Everybody will select three different numbers, even though that was not the question. When playing paper-scissors-rock people will also avoid using the same answer multiple times in a row. With that knowledge the average score can be improved.

Lets assume your opponent selected rock, and for that reason decides next time not to select rock. The average score table now looks like this:

		opponent			my score
		paper	rock	scissors	(average)
your move	paper	1	-	0	1/2
	rock	0	-	2	2/2
	scissors	2	-	1	3/2

The best average score is obtained if you select scissors. So based on your opponent's last move, there is always one move that gives you an advantage.

Software

This program is based on this technique. That does pose a bit of a problem: a player that does pick the same choice repeatedly will always win. And that would also be a pattern that people recognize quickly. So the program has one extra rule which means that if the program loses it will not make the same move again.

-- sanity check if my move is the same and you
-- won last time I make another move
if MyMove == MyLastMove & Iwin == 0 then
    MyMove = Yourmove + 1
    if MyMove > 3 then MyMove = 1 end if
end if

The program doesn't contain anything else worth discussing. You find the complete source in the download package.

Hardware

The schematic and the picture of the breadboard can be used to build this project.

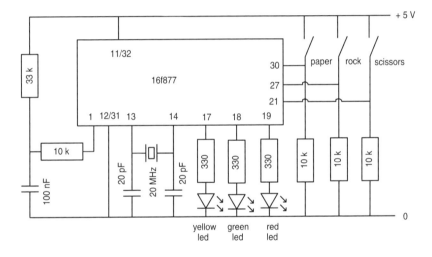

Figure 7. Paper-scissors-rock schematic.

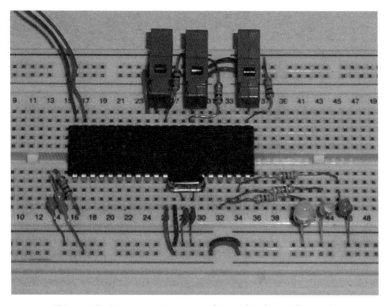

Figure 8. Paper-scissors-rock on the breadboard.

Instructions

Built the project and download the JAL program to the microcontroller. If in doubt check the tutorial project to see how this should be done. After downloading the yellow LED will light for a short moment: this is your cue to make a move.

The three switches on the breadboard represent from left to right scissors, rock and paper. Make your choice and press the respective button. The microcontroller will also make a choice and show the result using the LEDs:

Color	Meaning
yellow	draw
green	you win
red	you loose

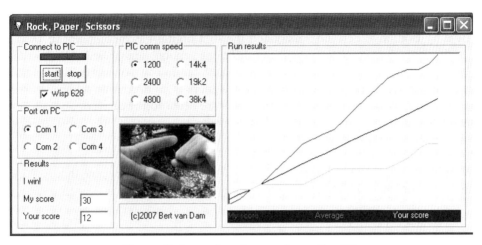

Figure 9. Reporting the results on the PC.

In the download package you will find a Visual Basic program which will keep track of the score, both in a counter as well as in a graph. If you want to use this program you should not remove the Wisp programmer when you're done programming. Start the Visual Basic program, check if the correct COM port has been selected and click on "Start" in the "Connect to PIC" rectangle. During play the scores are automatically kept. Always switch the microcontroller on before clicking on "Start" on the PC.

Optional 1

It does make a difference if you watch the graph on the PC screen during play. The most honest results are obtained when you do not look at the screen until you're done. That way you will exclusively make use of the pattern recognition capabilities of your brain.

Optional 2

What would be the effect if during play you show a wrong graph, and only show the correct one after the game has been terminated? Would this wrong graph be so misleading that you would obtain a statistically different result?

2.2 The last pebble

On the table lies a stack of identical objects, such as pebbles. Two players take turns removing a number of pebbles from the stack. The last player to take a pebble loses. In each turn 1,2 or 3 pebbles may be taken.

This game, called "Nim", is very old. In 1902 Nim was analyzed scientifically for the first time by Bouton[15]. Ferranti[16] marketed the first digital game computer in 1951 with Nim as the (only) game. Nowadays many different versions are played. The best known may be one where the pebbles are not on one stack but in rows of increasing length. The rule is to take at least one pebble from one row. There is no maximum number of pebbles that one can remove. Nowadays Moore's[17] rules are often followed were one can remove pebbles from multiple rows. If the players make no mistakes the game theory can accurately predict who will win.

The Nim game, which is used here, can also be predicted using the game theory. You win if your opponent leaves n pebbles for you, assuming that [18]:

$$n \bmod 4 = 1$$

Let's say it is your turn to play, and there are 6 pebbles left.

possible move	left over (n)	n mod 4
1	5	5 mod 4 = 1
2	4	4 mod 4 = 0
3	3	3 mod 4 = 3

So you have to chose option one and remove one pebble. That leaves five pebbles, and it is easy to see that no matter what your opponent does you always win.

It is not so difficult to incorporate this in a computer program. We have opted however for a completely different technique. One that is more in line with the way people try learn how to play this game.

Let's assume again that six pebbles are left on the table. You pick two, so that leaves four for your opponent. Your opponent takes three, leaving one for you. So you lose. The lesson learned is that next time you won't leave four pebbles for your opponent anymore.

---

[15] Bouton, C. L. (1902), "Nim, A Game with A Complete Mathematical Theory," *Annals of Math,* Vol. 3, pp. 35-39

[16] The Ferranti Nimrod Digital Computer, Faster than Thought, Science Exhibition at the Festival of Britain, May 5th, 1951.

[17] Moore, E. H. (1910), "A Generalization of the Game Called Nim," *Annals of Math.,* Vol. 11, pp. 93-94.

[18] Mod is short for modulo, and literally means size. It is the remainder after a division. For example 9/4 equals 2 with remainder 1. So 9 mod 4 = 1.

If in the next game you face the same situation with six pebbles on the table you will remove one or three but definitely not two. If you take three you will lose again. Yet another move not to make in the future.

So eventually, when confronted with six pebbles, you will remove only one (and win):

six pebbles remain	possible move	experience
	1	
	2	don't do this
	3	don't do this

This is the technique that we will use in our program. We will start with 21 pebbles. All possible moves are stored in memory as an array. The value of each move can be 0 ("don't do this") or 1 ("no opinion yet"). So the previous table would look like this in an array:

$$(6,1) = 1$$
$$(6,2) = 0$$
$$(6,3) = 0$$

Software

JAL doesn't have two-dimensional arrays so we will store the data sequentially. We opt for the EEPROM memory of the 16F877 because this is permanent memory. That means the microcontroller will remember what it has learned, even when it is switched off.

```
-- prepare the data array
column = 0
row = 0
for 21 loop
    row = 0
    column = column +1
    for 3 loop
        row = row +1
        if column > row then
            data_eeprom_write((row-1)*maxcol+column+startpnt, 1)
        else
            data_eeprom_write((row-1)*maxcol+column+startpnt, 0)
        end if
    end loop
end loop
```

There is sufficient room in EEPROM (in fact 256 bytes) so we will make our live easy by storing all combinations, even those that are impossible, such as (2,3), (1,2), and (1,3). This makes retrieving a combination very simple.

```
for 3 loop
    row = row +1
    data_eeprom_read((row-1)*maxcol+current+startpnt, answer)
    if answer == 1 then
        mymove = row
    end if
end loop
```

The impossible combinations are given the value 0 ("don't do this") which prevents them from being selected. The game starts with 21 pebbles, and it is your turn.

Hardware

The schematic and the picture of the breadboard can be used to build this project.

If your LCD screen is blank or filled with nothing but black blocks use the variable resistor to adjust the brightness. The switch can be used to switch the backlight of the LCD screen on.

When you use a display that is incompatible with the 44780 standard you will need to use a different JAL library.

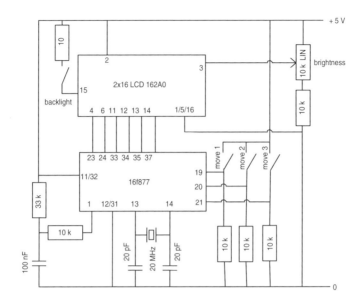

Figure 10. Nim schematic.

Figure 11. The Nim game in action.

Instructions

The game starts with 21 pebbles, and it is your turn. That means the microcontroller can always win, assuming it makes no mistakes. Initially this is most certainly not the case so you won't have any trouble winning. But as time progresses winning gets more and more difficult and eventually you will consistently lose

Switching the microcontroller off and on will not erase the microcontrollers knowledge because it is stored in EEPROM memory. If you want to start with an empty memory again you need to reload the program in the microcontroller using the Wisp programmer.

You can pick pebbles by pressing the buttons. On the breadboard the left button is used to pick one pebble, the middle button is used to pick two pebbles, and the right button is used to pick three pebbles.

Optional 1

There is sufficient EEPROM memory to start with more pebbles, in fact to a maximum of 85[19]. If you add a multiples of 4 to the current starting value of 21 the microcontroller can (after training) always win. In all other cases you can always win. Whether you can actually succeed in doing this remains to be seen!

Optional 2

You can also opt to write a program that uses the game theory to win as explained in the preamble. Based on the starting value you know in advance if the microcontroller can win. The program could bet with the human player on who wins or loses. Of course this has nothing to do with artificial intelligence, but the human player will start to wonder how the microcontroller always knows who wins.

Mind you: the fact that the human player can win doesn't necessarily means that he will indeed win. He will still need to make zero mistakes.

---

[19] For each move you need three bytes in the table, and the EEPROM has 256 bytes available.

3   Emerging behavior

Everyone who has been to a European soccer game has seen "The Wave". It's a wave of people who stand up, throw their arms high up in the air, and then sit down again. By doing that one after the other the wave of people standing up seems to move around the stadium.

At first glance it appears as if an invisible director choreographs this wave so that everyone stands up at the correct moment. In reality that doesn't happen. The spectators just follow a set of simple rules:

  1. I see the person next to me getting up.
  2. So I get up too.
  3. I throw my arms momentarily in the air.
  4. And then I sit down again.

Since everyone follows the exact same (simple) rules a special kind of group behavior emerges. This is called Emerging Behavior. The phenomena was first discovered by Keller and Segel[20] during their research into a type of fungus which as a group appeared to exhibit a certain behavior. As it turns out this phenomenon is actually quite common and can be found in many unexpected places such as anthill or the location of shops in a city[21]. Even the gracious movements of a flock of birds can be explained this way.

3.1   The electronic wave

The electronic equivalent of a wave is of course a running light. It would be quite simple to take a 16F877 and program it with a running light, but instead we will take four tiny microcontrollers, the 12F675, and give each one an eye to look with (an LDR) and a light to set (an LED).

Each 12F675 will also get the exact same program that exhibits the same behavior as people participating in a wave.

  1. I see that the LED of the module next to me is on.
  2. So I will light mine too.
  3. I will leave it on for a bit.
  4. And then switch I it back off.

---

[20] E. F. Keller and J. A. Segel. Initiation of slime mold aggregation viewed as an instability. J. Theor. Biology, 26:399-415, 1970
[21] S. Johnson, Emergence, the connected lives of ants, brains, cities and software, Scribner 2001, ISBN0-684-86875-x

Of course in this situation nothing will happen because non of the modules will start the sequence. And should for some reason a wave actually start it would never stop. So we will need to add two more rules.

5. Sometimes I light my LED for no apparent reason.
6. Sometimes I get bored and stop.

Software

Research done by Farkas[22] has shown that only a few dozen people are required to start a real wave in a stadium. Once started it will reach a speed of about 12 meters per second. Each spectator has a reaction time of about 0.5 seconds to realize that the person next to him got up. The time required to make the wave motion is about 8 seconds. In our electronic situation that doesn't look very appealing, so we will use a reaction time of 0.2 seconds an LED "on" time of 0.1 second (*ontime*).

The sensitivity of the LDRs needs to be adjusted whenever the amount of ambient light changes, otherwise it won't notice the LED of the neighbor unit going on. It would be impossible to do this manually for all units, so the program contains an auto calibration section.

```
-- take a sample
resist = ADC_read_low_res(2)

-- get a random value
randomval = random_byte

-- check if a light has been observed by the LDR
-- and if so turn on the own light after a short delay
if resist < threshold then
    -- see if you feel like participating
    if randomval > 50 then
        senddata
        delay_10ms( reactiontime )
        ledon
    end if
end if
```

---

[22] Farkas, I., D. Helbing, and T. Vicsek. 2002. Mexican waves in an excitable medium. Nature 419 (Sept. 12):131-132.

```
-- calculate new threshold value
threshold = resist / 10
threshold = threshold * 9
```

In this code fragment the resistance of the LDR (Light Dependent Resistor) is measured and stored in the variable *resist*. The next step is to check if this value is below the current threshold (*threshold*). If so the unit can decide to participate in the wave, the chance of doing so is 80%.

As a next step the threshold is re-determined. Because *threshold* is defined as a byte, and bytes can not be larger than 255 an elaborate calculation is used to set the *threshold* to 90% of the current measurement. By using the auto calibration gradual changes in the ambient light intensity have no effect on the units.

Hardware

The schematic and the picture of the breadboard can be used to build the required hardware. In this project four units are used. The LDR and LED of adjacent units are placed close together to prevent short cuts in the loop. Of course you can built more units and make the circle larger.

All 12F675 microcontrollers receive the exact same program. Since this is the first time the 12F675 is used the following table shows how to connect the programmer wires:

wire color	connect to
yellow	pin 4
blue	pin 7
green	pin 6
white	not used
red	+5 volt
black	0

If you use the Wisp628 you need a special dongle in order to program the 12F675. The schematic of this dongle can be found in appendix 12.3. If you use the Wisp648 the dongle is not required, but you do need to set the jumper (remember to remove the jumper before programming other microcontrollers)

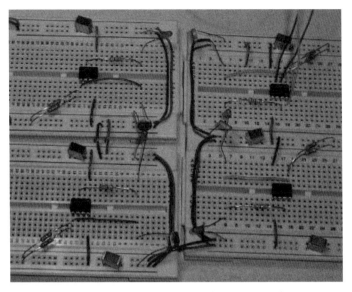

Figure 12. Four units placed close together.

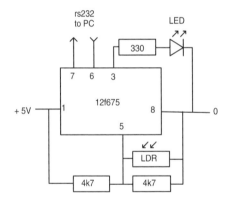

Figure 13. A single unit.

When you switch on the units you will observe a bizarre phenomena. Sometimes nothing will happen, then suddenly a flashing LED circles around, to extinguish unexpectedly moments later. At other moments two or three waves may start at the exact same time, resulting in a mayhem of flashing LEDs.

Optional 1

In this project the 12F675 units are placed in a circle. An alternative would be to use different configurations, for example all in one line. By changing the program you can then make all sorts of running lights and flashing lights.

Optional 2

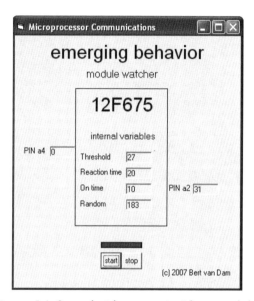

Figure 14. See what happens inside a module.

In the download package you will find a small Visual Basic program which will allow you to look inside one of the units. When you program the last microcontroller simply leave the Wisp wires in place and start this program. It will activate the pass-through functionality of the Wisp programmer. The interesting thing about this is that you can see the auto calibration in action. Play with the ambient light level and see what happens to the threshold. All units have the exact same program so it doesn't make any difference to which module you connect the programmer.

3.2   The Ant path

When ants are looking for food they wander around until they find something to eat. They take (part of that) food back to the nest, and leave behind a trail of a chemical scent called pheromone[23]. When other ants follow this trail it will led them to the food too. On

---

[23] Actually several different kinds of pheromone exist, for example for sex, following trails and to mark territories. In the context of ants one usually refers to the scent for following trails.

returning to the nest with food they too leave a trail, thus making it ever stronger. Once all the food is gone no new pheromone will be added, so the trail will evaporate. The ants will now start to randomly wander about again. This behavior can be observed in the simulation program by Maturana[24].

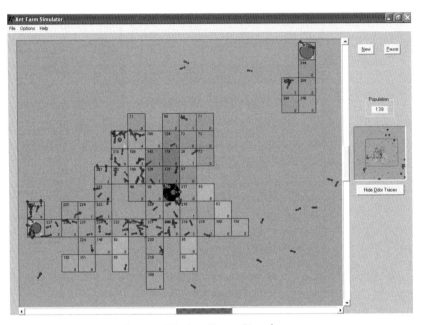

Figure 15. Ant Farm Simulator.

In this program the green circle represents food, the black circle represents the entrance to the nest, and the green squares indicate the pheromone trail.

Now let's assume the ants can follow two different paths, each with a different length. It will take the ants on the longer path more time to get back to the nest than the ones on the shorter path. So the scent they leave behind gets more time to evaporate than on the shorter path. So when an equal amount of ants would follow the two paths the shortest path would be the one with the strongest scent, and it would thus attract more ants. This means most ants will eventually follow the shortest path. They do this without any knowledge about the environment, and without deliberation: clearly emerging behavior.

---

[24] Maturana, RA, http://www.geocities.com/chamonate/hormigas/antfarm/, Ant Farm Simulator, 2004, the source code has been made available for readers of this book free of charge.

Dorigo[25] has named this technique ACO (Ant Colony Optimization algorithm). It turns out that it can be used quite easily for all sorts of optimizations such as of course the determination of the shortest path between two locations.

This technique works fine in itself, but it is a bit more complicated than just a pheromone trail. In reality ants have an excellent sense of direction. The first ant to find food has no trouble whatsoever to find the entrance of the nest, and not necessarily by backtracking over the path it used to find the food in the first place[26]. Exactly how ants do this is not known. It is clear however that the environment of the nest (such as overhanging branches) plays a roll of some sort[27].

A navigation system like this is necessary. Without it the ants could quite easily walk around in circles, or follow a trail in the wrong directing and never make it back to the nest.

To avoid this problem in simulations different techniques are used. For example an ant is only allowed to lay a pheromone trail once he has reached the target successfully. In this project we will try to mimic the actual ant behavior as much as possible. An ant carrying no food will not lay a pheromone trail and may only chose paths leading away from the nest. Once it has food found it may only chose paths that lead in the general direction of the nest. The paths that have been used most often (and thus carry the strongest pheromone trail) have the highest chance of being selected again. This applies to both outward and inward bound moving ants. This would appear to be the cleanest simulation model.

In this project a simulation environment has been made with an anthill, a location with food, and five junctions where an ant can make a decision as to which path to follow (see the next Figure). Six of the multitudes of routes that can be followed when travelling from the nest to the food are shown. In theory other routes are possible, but given the ants sense of direction these are not very likely.

---

[25] Dorigo, M, cs, Ant Algorithms for Discrete Optimization, Artificial Life, Vol. 5 nr 2 MIT Press, 1999.
[26] Shen, JX, cs, Direct homing behaviour in the ant Tetramorium caespitum (Formicidae, Myrmicinae), Animal Behaviour, Volume 55, Number 6, June 1998 , pp. 1443-1450(8)
[27] Harris, RA, cs, Ant navigation: Priming of visual route memories, Nature 438, 302 (17 November 2005)

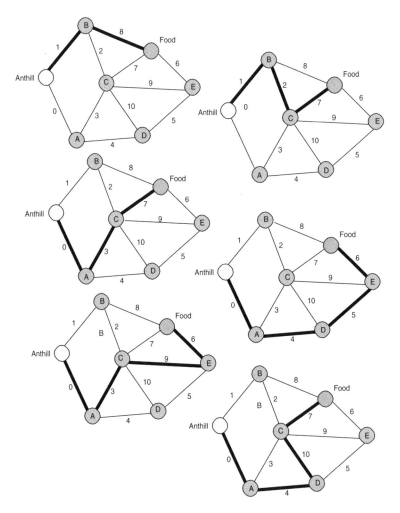

Figure 16. Possible routes between anthill and food.

The JAL program works as follows. All ants start in the nest. The are inclined to walk to the right (away from the nest) but are free to follow any route they want. At each junction a choice is made based on the amount of pheromone on the different paths. The path with the most pheromone has the highest chance of being selected. This choice is made using the roulette wheel selection technique, which is discussed in detail in the next chapter. At this point we will take for granted that this mechanism exists.

The ant data is stored in two arrays. One of the arrays keeps track of the location of the ant ("AntLocation"), the other one of whether the ant is carrying food or not ("AntFood").

For each ant the data is gathered from the arrays, and based on this the next step of the ant is determined:

```
-- retrieve ant data
Location = AntLocation[Ant]
Food = AntFood[Ant]
```

The possible paths that the ant can follow are also stored in an array ("WorldPath"). The value stored with each path indicates the amount of pheromone on it. For each location or junction (depicted by a circle in the figure) the program keeps track of which other junctions can be reached from that junction and how to get there.

The following program snippet shows as an example what happens at location 0 (the nest)

```
If Location == 0 Then
    -- ant hill
    Pheromone = WorldPath[0]  + WorldPath[1]
    Choice = (word(random_byte) * word(Pheromone))/255
    If Choice < WorldPath[0]  Then
        Path = 0
        NewLocation = 2
    Else
        Path = 1
        NewLocation = 3
    End If
    -- drop off any food
    Food = 0
End If
```

Using the roulette wheel mechanism *Choice* is used to make a choice from the possible paths to follow. Food, if any, is left behind in the nest.

This line might surprise you:

```
Choice = (word(random_byte) * word(Pheromone))/255
```

Choice is defined as a word[28]. This is necessary because both *random_byte* and *Pheromone* are bytes. If these are multiplied the answer will not fit in a byte, but it will fit in a word. It is not enough to simply define *Choice* as a word, we also need to tell the JAL compiler that we insist on getting word as an answer. This can be done by marking

---

[28] A word is 16 bits, so it is 0 to 65.535, a byte is 8 bits so it is 0 to 255.

both bytes as a *word()*. Note that you will need to do this every time when the answer of a calculation is larger than the definition of the variables used in that calculation.

The other junctions look similar. On most locations (except the Anthill and Food) the choice of the Ant is influenced by his sense of direction. This is maintained in the variables *ToFood* and *ToAnthill*.

```
Food = AntFood[Ant]
If Food == 1 Then
     ToAnthill = 1
     ToFood = 0
Else
     ToAnthill = 0
     ToFood = 1
End If
```

If the ant is carrying food he is obviously on its way to the nest, so *ToFood* is zero and *ToAnthill* is one. In the next formula taken from location A the "wrong" direction is therefor always multiplied by zero and therefor has no influence on the decision to be made.:

Pheromone=WorldPath[0]*ToAnthill+WorldPath[3]*ToFood+WorldPath[4]*ToFood

If for example the ant just came from the nest then he won't be able to select path 0, because that would lead him straight back.

When the route is determined the pheromone trail is adjusted accordingly:

```
-- adjust Pheromone trail
If Food == 0 Then
    WorldPath[Path]  = WorldPath[Path]  + 0
Else
    WorldPath[Path]  = WorldPath[Path]  + 5
End If
```

If the ant is not carrying any food no pheromone trail is deposited. Strictly speaking the first part of this statement is not really needed. Even the variables *ToAnthill* and *ToFood* could be used in a simpler way. Using this slightly more elaborate way however gives you a chance to play with these settings and observe their effect.

The only thing left is to slowly let the pheromone trail evaporate, as shown in the next snippet.

38

-- Pheromone decay

```
For 11 using Path loop
    serial_sw_write (Path)
    Border = (30 * word(WorldPath[Path]) /100)
    If Border == 0 Then
        WorldPath[Path] = 1
    Else
        WorldPath[Path] = Border
    End If
    serial_sw_write(WorldPath[Path])
end loop
```

This is also the place where the data are being sent to the PC so you can see what is going on inside the microcontroller.

Hardware

The schematic and picture of the breadboard can be used to build this project. After programming leave the programmer wires connected. The Wisp programmer is a requirement for this project so you can observe the search for the shortest path on the PC.

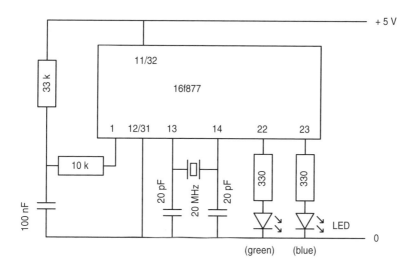

Figure 17. The antpath.

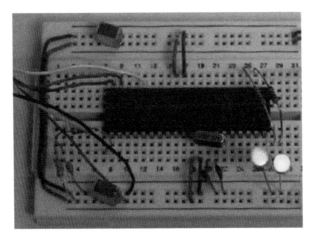

Figure 18. The antpath.

The long wires running to the left are from the Wisp programmer.

Instructions

Built the hardware and download the JAL program. Leave the Wisp programmer connected and start the Visual Basic program that you will find in the project directory. You will see a graphical representation of the ant's world. The yellow circle on the left is the anthill, the green circle more or less on the right is the food source. The numbers near the paths are identical to the numbers you've seen in the JAL program

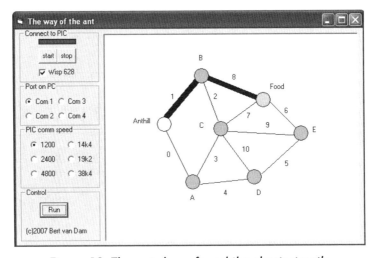

Figure 19. The ants have found the shortest path.

Check if the correct COM port has been selected and click on "Start" in the "Connect to PIC" frame. The rectangle will become green. Now click on "Run" in the "Control" frame. On the breadboard the two LED will flash alternatingly to indicate that the program is running.

In the ant world on the screen some lines will become wider and others thinner. The thickness of the line is an indication for the amount of pheromone on that particular path. The wider the line the more pheromone is on that path. As time progresses a pattern will emerge. When the microcontroller is done the LEDs will stop flashing and the rectangle near the "Start" button will turn red again. The path that was most used by the ants due to the high pheromone content is now clearly visible. In most cases this will indeed be the shortest route.

Optional 1

Due to the way the JAL program is constructed it is easy to play with its variables. What would for example happen if:

- The ants would leave a pheromone trail at all times?
- The ants have no sense of direction?
- The ants can drop food at other locations than the nest, and other ants can pick up that food?
- At the start of the program a "wrong" pheromone trail is already present?
- The pheromone evaporates quicker (or slower)?

Perhaps you need to increase the number of simulation runs to get a reliable result. The JAL program has one hundred simulation runs and that is quite short, you may want to increase that to one thousand or even more:

> *-- Do 100 simulations*
> for 100 using counter loop

Optional 2

Experienced Visual Basic programmers could change the ant's world, for example to make more paths, or use multiple food supplies, or food supplies that can run out of food.

4   Roulette wheel brain

Roulette wheel selection is technique that is used to make decisions mainly in the field of Genetic Algorithms (see chapter 7). The official name is stochastic sampling with replacement[29]. This technique is also very suitable for designing self-learning programs[30]. Roulette wheel is of course an incorrect term because roulette is the French word for a (small) wheel. It is however the common name for this technique so we will use it too.

Let's assume there are three possible choices to be made, A, B en C, and that each of them is equally likely. If we were to put these three choices on a roulette wheel it would look like the wheel on the left side of the picture below. All sections are the same size, so if you spin the wheel often enough each option will be selected equally often.

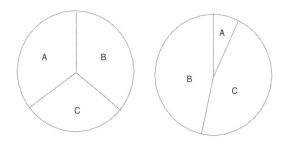

Figure 20. Roulette wheel before and after adaptation.

If for some reason section A would be made smaller choice A would be made less often, but choice B and C would be made more often. So by changing the size of the section for a particular option, the chance of that option being selected is also influenced. This sounds very obvious, and of course it is. But it does mean that the decision making process can be influenced in an extremely simple way. All you need to do is assign a value to each option that is equivalent to the size of the section on the roulette wheel for that option. If you increase the value, you also increase that chance of selection.

In theory it is possible to do the exact same thing by working with chances right from the start. In the left roulette wheel the chance of selection option A is 1/3, because:

[29] James E. Baker. Reducing Bias and Inefficiency in the Selection Algorithm, in Proceedings of the Second International Conference on Genetic Algorithms and their Application (Hillsdale), pp. 14-21, 1987.
[30] van dam, Self-learning wall avoider, Artificial Intelligence and Machine Learning, 1999, members.home.nl/b.vandam/robots/index.html

$$P_A = \frac{\text{circle section A}}{\text{circle section A} + \text{circle section B} + \text{circle section C}}$$

The difficulty is in the denominator. Each time we want to change the chance of option A, we need to know the chances of B and C as well. That would involve more calculations, and those take time. Time we may not have in mobile robot applications. If the roulette wheel technique is used the chances of B and C are not important. In fact it doesn't even matter if there actually are a B and C, or maybe also a D, or maybe just A. The only thing that matters at this point is that the value for A exists and that it needs to be a bit larger or smaller. This value is also called fitness[31]. This fitness can now be modified without the need for extensive calculations. Only when the fitness will actually be used are mathematics required.

Computers of course don't use a wheel, they simply place all fitnesses in a row, as shown in the next Figure.

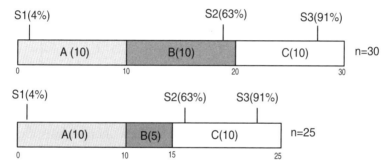

Figure 21. The reality of Roulette wheel selection.

In the upper bar A, B and C all have the same fitness (just like in the left picture in the roulette wheel Figure), namely 10. We will now make three random draws. Each draw is a percentage.

---

[31] Fitness literally means "The state or condition of being fit; suitability or appropriateness", in biology "The extent to which an organism is adapted to or able to produce offspring in a particular environment" from: The American Heritage® Dictionary of the English Language, Fourth Edition copyright ©2000 updated in 2003. Published by Houghton Mifflin Company.

draw	result (%)
1	4
2	63
3	91

The choice that goes with these percentages can be determined by adding up all possible fitnesses ("n" in the previous Figure) and multiply this with a percentage. For the upper bar the sum of the fitnesses is 30. The second draw from the table, 63% would in this case result in 63% x 30 = 18,9. According to that same upper bar this would be in area B (for B runs from 10 to 20). This is what the result for all draws looks like:

draw	result (%)	choice
1	4	A
2	63	B
3	91	C

Now assume that for some reason the fitness of option B is reduced from 10 to 5. The result is the lower bar in the previous figure. For draw number two the number now becomes 63% x 25 = 15,75. According to the lower bar this is in area C, for area C now runs from 15 to 25. This is the result for all draws:

draw	result (%)	choice
1	4	A
2	63	C
3	91	C

In the tutorial project this same technique was used. In that case there were only two choices: a green or a yellow LED. Each time when you rewarded the microcontroller the fitness of that color was increased, and the fitness for the other was decreased. Since there were only two options that was a simple application (particularly because the fitness sum was kept constant at 6), but it does show that this technique is very suited for autonomous learning programs.

4.1   Nothing in sight

Let's apply this technique in an autonomous learning robot. In the appendix you will find instructions on how to built this beautiful robot. In this project we will use two ultrasonic sensors[32] to observe the area in front of the robot, and two motors for propulsion[33].

The assignment given to this robot is to stay away from obstacles, in other word: no object may be in the sight of its ultrasonic sensors. So it is <u>not</u> the intention that the robot detects objects and tries to avoid them (this will be covered in chapter 5). The robot must find a behavior in which objects are simply never in sight of the sensors. You don't need a degree in robotics engineering to prevent the behavior this robot will need to display, but for the robot this assignment is far from easy.

The robot can chose from three possible actions:

- drive straight ahead
- turn left
- turn right

Note that the robot is not allowed to drive backwards because there are no sensors on the rear of the robot. Not moving at all by the way is also not an option for the robot, even though that would be a perfect solution for the problem at hand.

Software

At the start the roulette wheel is initialized by assigning fitness 10 to all possible actions. At this point as far as the robot is concerned each action is equally suited (or unsuited).

From now on every two seconds a random choice (called *wheel*) is made from these three actions using the roulette wheel. This way we avoid that the robot accidentally finds a suitable behavior and sticks with it without actually learning something.

Random_byte is a random number on byte[34] level. By dividing this by 255 we get a fraction between 0 and 1. Since a byte can only contain natural numbers we need to multiply this first by the sum of the fitness values!

---

[32] SRF04 Ultrasonic Range Finder.

[33] For autonomous robots it is essential to be round, and to be able to turn within their own circumference. This means that if one motor runs forward and the other is reversed the point of rotation of the robot is exactly in the center of its body. This way it will not get stuck when it hits something and tries to turn away.

[34] So between 0 and 255.

-- select an action using the roulette wheel
-- select a random number from the roulette wheel
wheel = (random_byte * (fitnessA + fitnessB + fitnessC))/255

The next step is to see which behavior belongs to this value. If there are no choices left to be made (*fitnessA + ftnessB + fitnessC* = 0) the robot will stop. It has in fact given up.

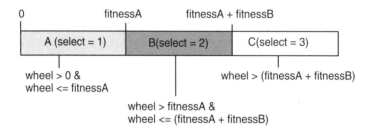

Figure 22. JAL roulette wheel selection.

The choices in the figure above look like this in JAL:

-- see in which action this number results
if (fitnessA + fitnessB + fitnessC) == 0 then select = 0 end if
if wheel > 0 & wheel <= fitnessA then select = 1 end if
if wheel > fitnessA & wheel <= (fitnessA + fitnessB) then select = 2 end if
if wheel > (fitnessA + fitnessB) then select = 3 end if

If an object is detected on one of the sensors the robot will backup for two seconds to release the sensors. If your robot is fast you may need to reduce that value to prevent it from backing into something. Because the assignment was that no objects may be seen it is not important which of the sensors saw the object. It is wrong no matter what, so backing up is the only option.

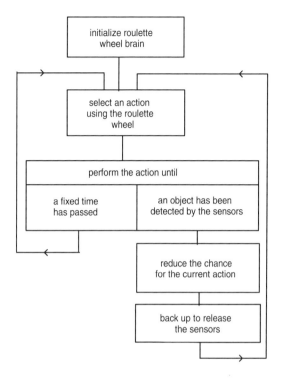

Figure 23. Schematic of the program execution.

The next step is to reduce the fitness of the action that resulted in the object coming within range of the sensors.

```
if Select ==  1 then
   if fitnessA >= 0 then
      fitnessA = fitnessA - 1
   end if
end if
if Select ==  2 then
   if fitnessB >= 0 then
      fitnessB = fitnessB - 1
   end if
end if
if Select ==  3 then
   if fitnessC >= 0 then
      fitnessC = fitnessC - 1
   end if
end if
```

Then a new choice is made. This process will repeat forever.

After trying a particular action (or rather: behavior) ten times unsuccessfully, the fitness will be zero, and that behavior will never be selected again. Ten is still quite often, and the robot looks a bit like a "naughty child" that keeps on trying things to see if it "can get away with it". Particularly if the fitness is low and the behavior is rarely selected.

Hardware

The schematic and the picture of the breadboard can be used to build this project. Of course you need to build the actual robot with control electronics (the motor control board) and the battery unit first. Instructions can be found in the appendix.

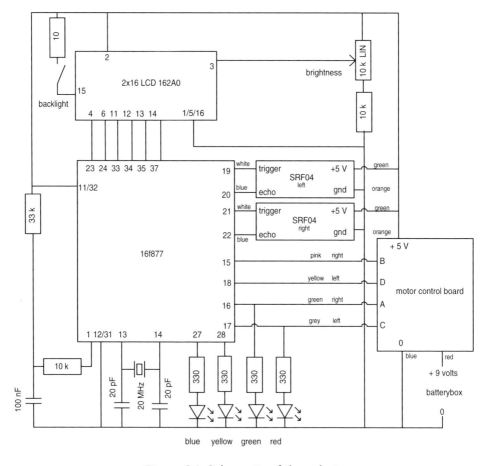

Figure 24. Schematic of the robot.

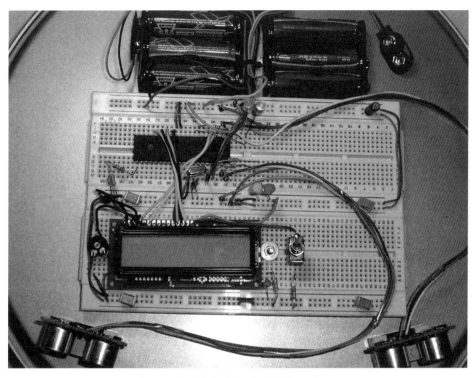

Figure 25. Nothing in Sight robot.

Instructions

Put the robot on the floor and switch it on. The LCD display shows the content of the roulette wheel brain. As soon as the robot detects an object it will backup for two seconds[35], reduce the fitness of this behavior and select a behavior from the available ones (note that this may very well be the exact same behavior that was just aborted).

If no object is detected the robot will make a new choice every two seconds, without backing up of course.

Eventually the robot will come to the conclusion that the only save behavior is turning. So after a while it will sit in one place and make turns more or less alternatingly left and right

---

[35] If your robot is fast you may want to reduce this time.

Optional

The best solution, not doing anything, was not an option for this robot. You could add this option to the program and see if the robot, with its tiny brain, will reach the same conclusion that you did.

You will see that this usually doesn't happen. The reason for this is that you find "doing nothing" the best solution because rocking from left to right in one place is "useless" in your opinion. Robots however don't have these emotions and are quite happy with any solution that meets the criteria, even if that involves repeating the same movement over and over again.

Perhaps you could re-write the program and make energy consumption a consideration when evaluating the fitness of a behavior. You could then reformulate the assignment so that nothing should be visible on the sensors while at the same time the energy consumption should be as low as possible.

5 Neural network

In 1906 Cajal[36] received the Nobel Prize for his discovery that our brain consists of neurons which are connected to each other by dendrites. It will take until 1949 before Hebb[37] discovers how humans and animals learn new things. It turns out that two separate mechanisms exist. First of all the brain can grow new dendrites that take care of new connections between neurons, which mainly takes place in the first years after birth. After that initial development stage learning mainly consists of strengthening of weakening the existing dendrite connections themselves.

Neural networks are an attempt to model the structure of our brain in a computer program. In this book we will use Hopfield[38] networks. These networks consist of a single layer, which means that all junctions are connected to the input as well as the output of signals. These junctions are the equivalent of the neurons in our brain, and thus they are usually called neurons. The main characteristic of a Hopfield network is that all neurons are connected to each other. These connections represent the dendrites in our brain. This figure shows a graphical representation of a Hopfield network.

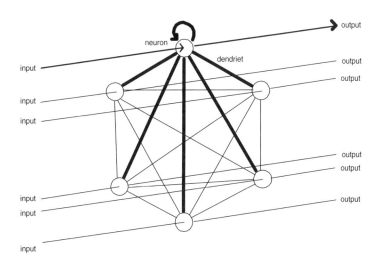

Figure 26. Hopfield 6x6 neural network.

[36] Ramón y Cajal, Santiago (1937). Recuerdos de mi Vida. Cambridge: MIT Press. ISBN 8420622907.
[37] The organization of behavior; a neuropsychological theory, Hebb, D.O. (1949), Wiley-Interscience, New York
[38] J. J. Hopfield, "Neural networks and physical systems with emergent collective computational abilities", Proceedings of the National Academy of Sciences of the USA, vol. 79 no. 8 pp. 2554-2558, April 1982.

A Hopfield network is associative, which means it works by associating the input with knowledge already in the brain to generate an output. Let us assume for example that you have learned to recognize the following Figure as the letter "b".

Figure 27. The letter b.

You probably did recognize it as the letter "b" because it is one. Interestingly enough you will recognize the letter "b" in the next Figure as well:

Figure 28. Black dots and stripes.

Of course this is not a "b" at all, but a group of black dots and stripes. Your brain however thinks that these dots and stripes show some resemblance to the letter "b", and since we were discussing letters a few moments ago it probably is in fact a "b". So your brain didn't recognize an actual "b", it just associated the dots and stripes pattern with a "b". This is an important difference, which will come in quite handy in the next projects.

Just as you had to learn the letter "b' first before you could recognize it, so has a neural Hopfield network. You can teach the network anything as long as it comes in a series of - 1 and +1 digits. Note that we are not using 0's and 1's as you might have expected! Let us assume you want the network to remember the following row of data: 1, -1, -1, -1, 1, 1 (what these data represent is totally irrelevant, at least to the network). In stead of writing them down in a row we will turn then into a vector:

$$\begin{pmatrix} 1 \\ -1 \\ -1 \\ -1 \\ 1 \\ 1 \end{pmatrix}$$

The vector needs to be turned into a matrix by multiplying it with itself. The easiest way to do this is to put the vector in a table, both above and on the left side, and multiply those with each other.

	1	**-1**	**-1**	**-1**	**1**	**1**
1	1 x 1 = 1	-1 x 1 = -1	-1 x 1 = -1	-1 x 1 = -1	1 x 1 = 1	1 x 1 = 1
-1	1 x –1 = -1	-1 x –1 = 1	-1 x –1 = 1	-1 x –1 = 1	1 x –1 = -1	1 x –1 = -1
-1	1 x –1 = -1	-1 x –1 = 1	-1 x –1 = 1	-1 x –1 = 1	1 x –1 = -1	1 x –1 = -1
-1	1 x –1 = -1	-1 x –1 = 1	-1 x –1 = 1	-1 x –1 = 1	1 x –1 = -1	1 x –1 = -1
1	1 x 1 = 1	-1 x 1 = -1	-1 x 1 = -1	-1 x 1 = -1	1 x 1 = 1	1 x 1 = 1
1	1 x 1 = 1	-1 x 1 = -1	-1 x 1 = -1	-1 x 1 = -1	1 x 1 = 1	1 x 1 = 1

Mathematicians would write this:

$$
\begin{pmatrix} 1 \\ -1 \\ -1 \\ -1 \\ 1 \\ 1 \end{pmatrix} \times \begin{pmatrix} 1 \\ -1 \\ -1 \\ -1 \\ 1 \\ 1 \end{pmatrix} = \begin{pmatrix} 1 & -1 & -1 & -1 & 1 & 1 \\ -1 & 1 & 1 & 1 & -1 & -1 \\ -1 & 1 & 1 & 1 & -1 & -1 \\ -1 & 1 & 1 & 1 & -1 & -1 \\ 1 & -1 & -1 & -1 & 1 & 1 \\ 1 & -1 & -1 & -1 & 1 & 1 \end{pmatrix}
$$

The Hopfield network already existed before we started with these calculations, but all connections still had value 0[39]. What we have in fact done is modify the strength of the connections between the different neurons, something that according to Hebb happens in humans and animals as well when they are learning something.

Let's take another row of data, for example 1, -1, 1, -1, 1, -1 and turn it into a matrix in exactly the same way.

$$
\begin{pmatrix} 1 \\ -1 \\ 1 \\ -1 \\ 1 \\ -1 \end{pmatrix} \times \begin{pmatrix} 1 \\ -1 \\ 1 \\ -1 \\ 1 \\ -1 \end{pmatrix} = \begin{pmatrix} 1 & -1 & 1 & -1 & 1 & -1 \\ -1 & 1 & -1 & 1 & -1 & 1 \\ 1 & -1 & 1 & -1 & 1 & -1 \\ -1 & 1 & -1 & 1 & -1 & 1 \\ 1 & -1 & 1 & -1 & 1 & -1 \\ -1 & 1 & -1 & 1 & -1 & 1 \end{pmatrix}
$$

---

[39] The rule that only +1 and -1 may be used applies to the data, not to the content of the network. The network itself may contain any possible value.

The next step is to add these matrices together. You can do this by adding each number in the matrix by the number that occupies the same location in the other matrix. So the top left number of the first matrix (1) is added to the top left number of the second matrix (1) to yield the top left number of the result matrix (1+1=2). Continuing this for the other numbers in the matrices yields this result:

$$
\begin{pmatrix}
1 & -1 & -1 & -1 & 1 & 1 \\
-1 & 1 & 1 & 1 & -1 & -1 \\
-1 & 1 & 1 & 1 & -1 & -1 \\
-1 & 1 & 1 & 1 & -1 & -1 \\
1 & -1 & -1 & -1 & 1 & 1 \\
1 & -1 & -1 & -1 & 1 & 1
\end{pmatrix}
+
\begin{pmatrix}
1 & -1 & 1 & -1 & 1 & -1 \\
-1 & 1 & -1 & 1 & -1 & 1 \\
1 & -1 & 1 & -1 & 1 & -1 \\
-1 & 1 & -1 & 1 & -1 & 1 \\
1 & -1 & 1 & -1 & 1 & -1 \\
-1 & 1 & -1 & 1 & -1 & 1
\end{pmatrix}
=
\begin{pmatrix}
2 & -2 & 0 & -2 & 2 & 0 \\
-2 & 2 & 0 & 2 & -2 & 0 \\
0 & 0 & 2 & 0 & 0 & -2 \\
-2 & 2 & 0 & 2 & -2 & 0 \\
2 & -2 & 0 & -2 & 2 & 0 \\
0 & 0 & -2 & 0 & 0 & 2
\end{pmatrix}
$$

We have now turned both rows of data into a single matrix. For mathematicians the end result is a matrix, for biologist it is a neural network. We will uses both these terms in this book. By following this technique you can add as many rows of data to the neural network as you like, You can even "amplify" certain rows of data by adding them more than once.

Now this is all very interesting (or maybe not) but the point is that the neural network can remember both rows of data. You can check this by multiplying one of the rows with the network, and see if it yields the same answer. You do this by turning the vector horizontally and multiplying each number of the vector with the corresponding number in the matrix, row by row. For the first row the calculation is:

$$1 \times 2 + -1 \times -2 + -1 \times 0 + -1 \times -2 + 1 \times 2 + 1 \times 0 = 8$$

This has to be repeated for each row. Mathematicians write it like this:

$$
\begin{pmatrix}
2 & -2 & 0 & -2 & 2 & 0 \\
-2 & 2 & 0 & 2 & -2 & 0 \\
0 & 0 & 2 & 0 & 0 & -2 \\
-2 & 2 & 0 & 2 & -2 & 0 \\
2 & -2 & 0 & -2 & 2 & 0 \\
0 & 0 & -2 & 0 & 0 & 2
\end{pmatrix}
\times
\begin{pmatrix}
1 \\ -1 \\ -1 \\ -1 \\ 1 \\ 1
\end{pmatrix}
=
\begin{pmatrix}
8 \\ -8 \\ -4 \\ -8 \\ 8 \\ 4
\end{pmatrix}
\underset{\text{normalized}}{=}
\begin{pmatrix}
1 \\ -1 \\ -1 \\ -1 \\ 1 \\ 1
\end{pmatrix}
$$

Please note an important final step: normalization. We already know that data must consist of either +1 or -1. So we normalize all numbers larger than zero[40] to +1, and all numbers less then zero to -1.

---

[40] What happens to the zero depends on the situation. In some cases normalizing it to +1 gives a good result, in other cases normalizing to -1 one is better. You will need to experiment with that,

You see that the answer is exactly the same as the question, and that means the network has remembered that row of data, or rather: that vector. This is equivalent with your recognition of the letter "b' in the first Figure, because it was exactly identical to the image you have learned in school. Fun, but not spectacular, there are easier ways to accomplish that.

But what would happen if we offer the network a "mutilated letter b", so if we make a mistake by leaving data out? Since data offered to Hopfield networks can only be +1 and -1 the equivalent of leaving data out is using a 0, a non-existing entity for the network. Lets do some serious damage to the data and offer the network 0, 0, 0, -1, 1, 1 in stead of 1, -1, -1, -1, 1, 1 and see what happens:

$$
\begin{pmatrix}
2 & -2 & 0 & -2 & 2 & 0 \\
-2 & 2 & 0 & 2 & -2 & 0 \\
0 & 0 & 2 & 0 & 0 & -2 \\
-2 & 2 & 0 & 2 & -2 & 0 \\
2 & -2 & 0 & -2 & 2 & 0 \\
0 & 0 & -2 & 0 & 0 & 2
\end{pmatrix}
X
\begin{pmatrix}
0 \\ 0 \\ 0 \\ -1 \\ 1 \\ 1
\end{pmatrix}
=
\begin{pmatrix}
4 \\ -4 \\ -2 \\ -4 \\ 4 \\ 2
\end{pmatrix}
\underset{\text{normalized}}{=}
\begin{pmatrix}
1 \\ -1 \\ -1 \\ -1 \\ 1 \\ 1
\end{pmatrix}
$$

The amazing conclusion is that the network, despite the serious damage we did to the data, still manages to associate this with the row of data it has learned before. Very impressive! This is called "converging of the network to a solution". Important to remember is that *a Hopfield network tries to recognize in the input something that* <u>*resembles the most*</u> *the data is has learned before. So not necessarily an exact fit.*

5.1   Hopfield 4 x 4 autonomous learning

Let's put this into practice. We will build a robot with two sensors, which will use a neural network to avoid obstacles[41]. Note that this is an entirely different assignment as in chapter 4.1. That robot had to stay away from objects. This one may come close to objects as long as it doesn't hit any. An important difference, and you will see that it leads to totally different behavior.

---

neural networks are not an exact science yet. Once you pick a normalization you must stick with it for that particular network.

[41] A modern version of van Dam, KIJK November 1999, page 70.

Figure 29. Exploring the garden.

The number of data that this robot has access to is four, which we will put into vector like this:

>sensor left
>sensor right
>motor left
>motor right

An obvious choice would be a 4x4 Hopfield network. The vectors may only contain values +1 and -1 so we will agree that these have the following meaning:

>+1 motor on / sensor has not detected an object
>-1 motor off / sensor has detected an object

The best way not to hit anything would be not to move, but that is not the intention. At least not our intention. It remains to be seen whether the robot, while learning, cares to agree with us. The first vector to add to the network is:

$$\begin{pmatrix} 1 \\ 1 \\ 1 \\ 1 \end{pmatrix}$$

Which means: if the sensors have not detected any objects simply move straight ahead. That is a rule even the robot can't object to. It would be easy to design the other rules, turn them in vectors and add them to a network, but perhaps it is more fun to let the robot do this itself. Since we have no intention to run around behind the robot telling it which decision is wrong (and should not be learned) and which is right (and should be learned) we will let the robot handle that itself too. Truly autonomous learning. For that we need to mechanisms:

1. The robot must be able to try random behavior.
2. The robot must be able to differentiate between right and wrong behavior.

The first mechanism is easy to realize by simply switching motors on and off randomly. To prevent the robot from getting stuck reversing is not allowed, because there are no sensors at the rear. Turning has to be done by running one motor forward and one in reverse so the robot will turn within it's own circumference. So in effect the robot can randomly chose from the following behaviors:

- move straight ahead
- turn left
- turn right
- stop

Differentiating between right and wrong behavior is more difficult. The only solution is to simply try what the robot came up with and see if it improves the situation. The definition of "improvement" is that the sensors no longer see an object. The risk is that the robot while experimenting tries a totally wrong move and hits something. Which is of course a normal part of the learning process: which child hasn't touched a hot stove despite all the warnings?

If the robot thinks that this particular behavior had improved the situation it is stored in the neural network as a solution to this situation. So in the future when confronted with this situation (or something rather similar) the robot will do exactly the same thing. This by the way is not necessarily the answer you had in mind. Your expectation is perhaps that the robot will explore your house. It is very well possible that this will indeed happen. But it is also possible that the robot will drive around your chair all day, or that it becomes confused during learning and keeps bumping into things.

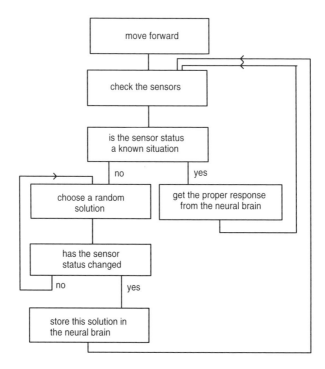

Figure 30. Program of the Hopfield 4x4 robot.

One important question remains. How does the robot know that a situation it encounters is indeed new? Every situation only results in sensor data, which is only part of the vector. Let us assume both sensors detect nothing. At this point we have no idea what the motors should do, so the associated vector would be:

$$\begin{pmatrix} 1 \\ 1 \\ 0 \\ 0 \end{pmatrix}$$

In the introduction we have seen that a Hopfield network can associate data with vectors it has learned before. So what would this vector yield as result?

$$\begin{pmatrix} 1 & 1 & 1 & 1 \\ 1 & 1 & 1 & 1 \\ 1 & 1 & 1 & 1 \\ 1 & 1 & 1 & 1 \end{pmatrix} \times \begin{pmatrix} 1 \\ 1 \\ 0 \\ 0 \end{pmatrix} = \begin{pmatrix} 2 \\ 2 \\ 2 \\ 2 \end{pmatrix} \text{ norm } \begin{pmatrix} 1 \\ 1 \\ 1 \\ 1 \end{pmatrix}$$

Please note that in the associated vector the sensor data (1,1) are identical to the original sensor input. We will assume that this means that the network has recognized the sensor data. That means that the resulting motor data (1,1) is the solution to this situation. In other words:

if the known data are correct we assume that the unknown data are also correct.

This is not necessarily true, this may also be a "false" memory". This matches the way the human brain works. Confronted with the question where you left your keys, the answer that comes to mind is usually, but not always, correct. We like to say we "misplaced" our keys, but in reality a false memory led us to the wrong location.

Software

The program for this robot is part of the download package. A few parts of it need to be discussed in a bit more detail. Lets start with the definition of the neural network and a vector:

```
-- Definition of the empty neural network,
-- where m stands for matrix
-- ( m1  m2  m3  m4 )
-- ( m5  m6  m7  m8 )
-- ( m9  m10 m11 m12 )
-- ( m13 m14 m15 m16 )

-- left bumper    ( v1 )
-- right bumper   ( v2 )
-- left motor     ( v3 )
-- right motor    ( v4 )
```

The next step is the matrix calculations (look up the variable names in the definition above to see how this is done):

```
procedure VectorTimesVector is
    -- Determine the resulting matrix if this vector
    -- is multiplied by itself. The formula of course is
    -- obvious (where nm stands for new matrix):
    nm1 = v1 * v1
    nm2 = v1 * v2
    nm3 = v1 * v3
    nm4 = v1 * v4
    nm5 = v2 * v1
```

```
        nm6 = v2 * v2
        nm7 = v2 * v3
        nm8 = v2 * v4
        nm9 = v3 * v1
        nm10 = v3 * v2
        nm11 = v3 * v3
        nm12 = v3 * v4
        nm13 = v4 * v1
        nm14 = v4 * v2
        nm15 = v4 * v3
        nm16 = v4 * v4
    end procedure

    procedure MatrixAddMatrix is
        -- To add this new knowledge to the neural network this
        -- matrix has to be added to the original one
        m1 = m1 + nm1
        m2 = m2 + nm2
        m3 = m3 + nm3
        m4 = m4 + nm4
        m5 = m5 + nm5
        m6 = m6 + nm6
        m7 = m7 + nm7
        m8 = m8 + nm8
        m9 = m9 + nm9
        m10 = m10 + nm10
        m11 = m11 + nm11
        m12 = m12 + nm12
        m13 = m13 + nm13
        m14 = m14 + nm14
        m15 = m15 + nm15
        m16 = m16 + nm16
    end procedure
```

Normalization means that you need to change positive vector values to +1 and negative vector values to -1. There is no general rule what needs to be done with zero. In this program a zero is normalized to -1.

```
        -- Normalize this vector by replacing anything
        -- larger than zero by +1 and anything smaller
        -- or equal to zero by -1
        If av1 > 0 Then av1 = 1 else av1 = -1 end if
        If av2 > 0 Then av2 = 1 else av2 = -1 end if
```

If av3 > 0 Then av3 = 1 else av3 = -1 end if
If av4 > 0 Then av4 = 1 else av4 = -1 end if

The software will send the content of the neural network to a PC. This is not necessary, but it is fun to see the content change during learning. You do need a very long wire, or a portable PC. If you do not want to keep the robot connected to the PC you do not need to change the program, simply reset the robot without the Wisp connected to it.

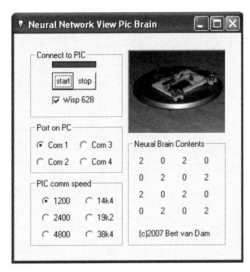

Figure 31. The content of the neural network.

Hardware

The schematic and the picture of the breadboard can be used to build this project. Note that you need to built the robot, the motor control section and the battery pack first, the instructions can be found in the appendix.

The LCD display is used to convey the status of the robot. The messages are:

Waiting

Unknown situation

Problem solved

Solution found

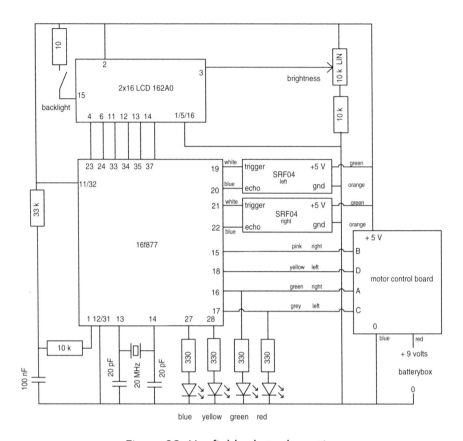

Figure 32. Hopfield robot schematic.

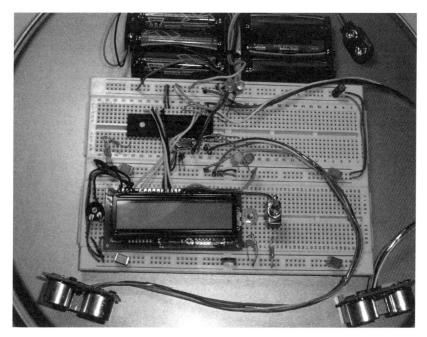

Figure 33. Hopfield robot electronics

Optional 1

Even though the results of autonomous learning are not predictable this robot usually learns to turn left if it detects an object on the right, and to turn right if it detects an object on the left. To human standards this is considered useful behavior. If an object is detected directly in front of the robot it will in that case stop and do nothing. This is in fact a false memory.

Since stopping and doing nothing is, to human standards, only funny if it accidentally happens directly in front of the TV, you could quite easily modify it by changing "stop" in the program by "turn left 4 seconds", like this:

```
if av3 == -1 & av4 == -1 then
     -- turn left 4 sec
     pin_c0 = 0
     pin_c1 = 1
     pin_c2 = 0
     pin_c3 = 1
     delay_1s(4)
end if
```

The program in the download package already has this modification. Note that 4 seconds may be to long (or short) for your robot, so adjust it as needed.

Optional 2

Another solution to this problem is to enlarge the neural network, for example to a 5x5 Hopfield. You could then use the following vector:

> object on left sensor only
> object on right sensor only
> object on both sensors
> motor left
> motor right

Optional 3

Since the robot is snooping around your house anyway why not give it a useful assignment my mounting a duster underneath to clean your parquet flooring.

5.2   Caenorhabditis Elegans

Since 1967[42] the just 1 mm long worm Caenorhabditis Elegans   (often lovingly abbreviated to C. Elegans) has been a source of interest to many scientists. This is because it has many of the organs that higher animals have too, but much simpler. Its short life span, just a few weeks, and his easy diet (plant remains in soil) make it an ideal research animal. The entire worm consists of just 959 cells, of which 302 are nerve cells.

Particularly interesting, considering the subject of this book, is that its brain consists of just 200 neurons[43]   (the human brain consists of approximately 100 billion neurons). Its brain is so small that it can be simulated quite nicely with a neural network.

---

[42] Nigon V, Brun J, Genetics and evolution of free nematodes. Perspectives deducted from the study of Caenorhabditis elegans, Experientia. 1967 Mar 15;23(3):161-70.
[43] J.G. White cs, Phil. Trans. Royal Soc. London. Series B, Biol Scien. Vol.314, Issue 1165 (Nov 12, 1986), 1-340

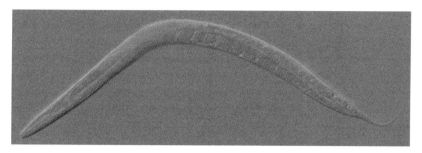

Figure 34. Caenorhabditis Elegans[44].

C. Elegans uses a wave-like motion to move forward, and a single chemical sensor to locate his food. If during the swinging motion of the sensor a particular direction yields a stronger signal, than that will be the preferred direction. For our robot we will use a light sensor instead of a chemical sensor, which means our robot will consider light to be a food source.

Even though C. Elegans is capable of learning (it can for example become nicotine addicted with the same withdrawal symptoms as human smokers[45]) we will make the network non-learning so we can set his behavior to mimic our worm as accurately as possible.

The following items will be in the vector:

> Light intensity at time 1
> Light intensity at time 0
> Radar Left
> Radar Right
> Motor Left
> Motor Right

In order to know if the robot is moving in the "right" direction, the light intensity will be sampled at regular intervals.

If for example at this moment (time 1) there is more light than the previous moment (time 0) the robot is most likely moving toward the light. So if there are no objects detected by the sensors it is best to move straight ahead. In this situation the vector would look like this:

---

[44] Photo Zeynep F. Altun, editor of www.wormatlas.org, licensed under the Creative Commons Attribution Share Alike License version 2.5: http://creativecommons.org/licenses/by-sa/2.5/

[45] Feng et al. (2006). A C. Elegans Model of Nicotine-Dependent Behavior: Regulation by TRP-Family Channels. Cell 127: 621-633.

vector	value	explanation
Light intensity at time 1	1	I see more light now...
Light intensity at time 0	-1	than a moment ago.
Radar Left	-1	no objects on the left radar
Radar Right	-1	no objects on the right radar
Motor Left	1	so move straight ahead
Motor Right	1	

With the following code for the vector values:

> +1 motor on / object detected / more (or the same amount of) light
> -1 motor off / no objects detected / less light

The behavior of the C. Elegans can be modeled as follows in vectors. Please note that not all possible options have been modeled, just the ones that seems most relevant,

vector	1	2	3	4	5	6	7	8	9	10
Light intensity at time 1	1	-1	1	-1	1	-1	1	1	1	1
Light intensity at time 0	-1	1	-1	1	-1	1	1	1	1	1
Radar Left	-1	-1	1	1	-1	-1	-1	-1	1	1
Radar Right	-1	-1	-1	-1	1	1	-1	1	-1	1
Motor Left	1	-1	1	1	-1	-1	1	-1	1	-1
Motor Right	1	1	-1	-1	1	1	1	1	-1	-1

Every vector needs to be multiplied with itself, and the resulting matrices need to be added together. This means we will end up with a 6x6 matrix, with 6 neurons. Much less than the 200 that the C. Elegans has, but much more efficiently interconnected.

Apart from that C. Elegans uses its brain for many more things than just figuring out in which direction it wants to move. So six neurons for just this decision might actually be quite close to reality. In any case this is the resulting network:

$$\begin{pmatrix} 10 & -2 & 0 & 0 & 2 & 0 \\ -2 & 10 & 0 & 0 & -2 & 0 \\ 0 & 0 & 10 & -2 & 4 & -10 \\ 0 & 0 & -2 & 10 & -8 & 2 \\ 2 & -2 & 4 & -8 & 10 & -4 \\ 0 & 0 & -10 & 2 & -4 & 10 \end{pmatrix}$$

In the download package you will find an Excel spreadsheet that you can use to check my calculations[46].

It is by the way still possible to write a more traditional type of program that has all the possible situation in a table. The program can simply search the table and select the proper solution. The main reason for using a neural network is that it is capable of finding solutions for situations that the robot designer never anticipated. Such as a stuttering sensor, or a crazy sensor reading because the robot is wobbling over an obstacle. It is these unexpected events that make writing robot software so difficult.

And then again it is possible that the robot would encounter a situation which is in itself valid, but is simply not in the table. A traditional program would stop, but let's see what the neural net will do, for example with this situation:

vector	content	explanation
Light intensity at time 1	1	I see more light now...
Light intensity at time 0	-1	than a moment ago, and
Radar Left	1	there is a object,
Radar Right	1	directly in front of me
Motor Left	0	
Motor Right	0	

Or: *the robot is moving towards the light when suddenly an object blocks the path.*

Note that this situation was not part of the network's training. This is the result:

Motor Left   -1
Motor Right   -1

In other words: stop. An excellent result!

---

[46] If you don't own Excel you may need to make the calculations manually. You could use the matrix functionality of the free calculator calc98: http://www.calculator.org/download.html

Software

Just like in the human brain different parts of the brain take care of different functionality:

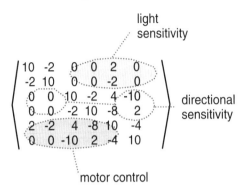

Figure 35. Functionality area's of the C. Elegans neural network.

For an autonomous learning robot it is important to know if a memory is true (so it can be used) or non-existent (so it needs to learn something new). In this case that is irrelevant. Right or wrong, the robot has to live with it. For that reason we only need to use that part of the network that is directly responsible for motor control (see the previous Figure), which is significantly smaller than the total network. Where m1 is the upper left corner of the matrix, m25 is the first matrix position in the motor control section:

-- define the brain (use the Excel spreadsheet to calculate these values)
m25= 2
m26= -2
m27= 4
m28= -8
m29= 10
m30= -4
m31= 0
m32= 0
m33= -10
m34= 2
m35= -4
m36= 10

The calculations are much simpler as well since only the motor control part is used:

```
-- process the vector in the neural brain to get motor data
v5 = m25 * v1 + m26 * v2 + m27 * v3 + m28 * v4
v6 = m31 * v1 + m32 * v2 + m33 * v3 + m34 * v4
```

It is of course possible that the brain comes to the conclusion that doing nothing is the proper action to take. As such there is nothing wrong with that idea. I'm sure C. Elegans would at times do the same thing. The robot reacts to changes in its environment, so chances are that since it's not moving the (perceived) environment is not changing much. So it may just sit there "forever". This is because the robot lacks a driver that C. Elegans has: hunger. So while at some point C. Elegans would start moving again, driven by the desire to find something to eat, the robot would not budge. If you want you can replace "standing still" by 4 seconds (or any other appropriate time) of turning, to avoid this situation. This is of course completely optional.

```
if v5 == -1 & v6 == -1 then
    -- turn left 4 sec
    pin_c0 = 0
    pin_c1 = 1
    pin_c2 = 0
    pin_c3 = 1
    delay_1s(4)
end if
```

Hardware

The schematic and the picture of the breadboard can be used to build this project. Of course you need to build the robot itself, the motor control electronics and the battery pack as per the instructions in the appendix.

The LCD display is used only to display the name of this robot: Caenorhabditis Elegans.

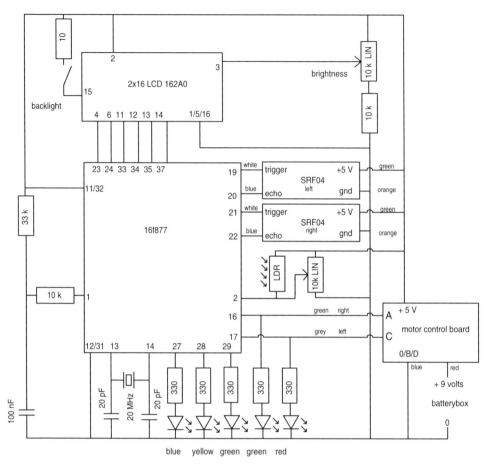

Figure 36. Schematic C. Elegans.

The most important changes compared to the previous project are:

1. The addition of an LDR on pin2.
2. The addition of three status LEDs.

The status LEDs more or less show the vector status, so you can observe what is going on.

color	function
red	motor left
green (next to red)	motor right
yellow	radar left
blue	radar right
green (next to blue)	LDR

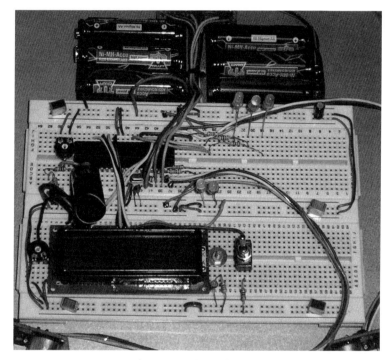

Figure 37. C. Elegans with additional components.

The LDR is encased in a black paper tube to make it direction sensitive, which works particularly well during the daytime. For my robot the 10k variable resistor over the LDR must be set about halfway. Because even "identical" LDRs can vary vastly in resistance your setting may be different.

Instructions

The content of the neural network is determined by the different vectors that were used to construct it. Even though only ten vectors were use the result is quite realistic.

Don't think that C. Elegans will rush towards the nearest light source, as we probably would. It is incapable of actively searching for the light, only when its swinging motion accidentally discovers the direction of the light source it can start moving in that general direction.

So it will be rummaging about to collect its food. At times it is quite happy to sit in one place and move back and forth for a quarter of an hour! Movies of the actual C. Elegans show similar behavior[47]. The sole exception is that the real worm will move forward in a wave, while our robot does this in a spiraling movement.

Optional

You can seriously modify the behavior of C. Elegans by using different vectors. Also interesting is to use fewer vectors, and see what the resulting behavior is. The first version of C. Elegans I ever built used just 6 vectors (and was already quite realistic), and I suspect less would also be possible.

In the download package you will find an Excel spreadsheet which will help you redesign the neural network. You start with entering the different vectors (the spreadsheet supports ten but can easily be expanded). With these vectors the matrix (so the neural net) is made automatically.

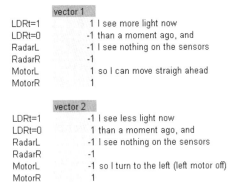

Figure 38. Entering vectors in the spreadsheet.

---

[47] Resources on the internet come and go but sometimes actual movies can be found.

Then you can enter test vectors to check the accuracy of the neural net you just designed. Your finished result can be copied directly from the spreadsheet to the JAL program

Neural Network Vector Calculations   Caenorhabditis Elegans   © 2007 Bert van Dam

neural brain content based on the vectors						testvector result	norm	function	direction
10	-2	0	0	2	0	1	12	1 LDRt=1	input
-2	10	0	0	-2	0	-1	-12	-1 LDRt=0	input
0	0	10	-2	4	-10	1	8	1 RadarL	input
0	0	-2	10	-8	2	1	8	1 RadarR	input
2	-2	4	-8	10	-4	0	0	-1 MotorL	output
0	0	-10	2	-4	10	0	-8	-1 MotorR	output

Instructions:

1. Enter the memory vectors in column B
2. Mark the outputs in columns P and S
3. Make all the outputs in column P '0' meaning we don't know what they should be
4. See if any crosses (wrong output) occur in colomn S
   (note that crosses outside this area have no impact, although technically memory retrieval is incorrect)
5. If yes: distribute in- and output differenty, or use a larger brain
   no : succes, the brain remembers all actions correctly
6. Optionally try non-memorized vectors in column AB to see what would happen if the brain encountered such an unknown situation
7. Use the table below to copy the brain to a JAL of VB program

Figure 39. Excel spreadsheet for neural networks.

6   Evolution

In 1859 Darwin wrote his famous book[48] "On The Origin of Species by Means of Natural Selection". After a careful and long study of nature he came to the conclusion that all living creatures are related to one another. In his opinion one species evolves from another by means of natural selection. Small random changes in looks or behavior that are an advantage to the creature in question (meaning that it has a better shot at reproduction) win the struggle for survival over members of that species that do not have that small advantage. Particularly his visit to the Galápagos islands, far away from the civilized world, with its own range of species and development convinced him of his opinion.

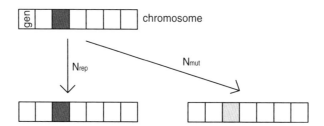

Figure 40. Reproduction and mutation.

The genes pass inheritable characteristics because they are copied into the next generation. A human child for example will get part of the genes of the father, and part of the genes of the mother, thus combining inheritable characteristics of both parents. While the genes are copied (or: reproduced), sometimes small random changes are made. These small changes are called mutations, a very poor choice of words, which suggests dramatic events and horrible disfigurations. Mutations aren't errors or accidents, but small changes that are a natural part of reproduction. They don't happen very often, in general the number of reproductions is far greater than the number of mutations.

$$N_{rep} \gg N_{mut}$$

Mutations cause tiny changes, for example the ability to see just a tiny bit better then your peers, or be just a tiny bit more resistant against antibiotics[49]. If this tiny change doesn't pose an advantage it will not have any influence. But if it does pose an advantage, particularly if it allows the bearer to have more or healthier offspring then this small

---

[48] On The Origin of Species by Means of Natural Selection, or the Preservation of Favoured Races in the Struggle for Life, John Murray, London, 1859

[49] Wojnicz D cs, Infectivity and resistance to antibiotics of bacterial strains isolated from patients hospitalized in intensive care units, Med Dosw Mikrobiol. 2007;59(1):75-84

change will gradually become the norm. This is because the bearer will have more offspring than the non-bearers, so after some generations everyone will be a bearer. It is this phenomenon that causes an increasing number of bacteria strains to be resistant against antibiotics.

In this case a certain small group of bacteria by pure chance was more resilient against the antibiotics (due to a small mutation during reproduction). So while their peers died quickly they were still alive and able to reproduce. Thus replacing dead non-bearers with live bearers. Eventually everyone alive was a bearer, and thus antibiotic resistance became a normal characteristic for this strain of bacteria. In places where antibiotics are not (often) used this characteristic would not be an advantage. For that reason particularly bacteria in hospitals have grown such a resistance[50].

Evolution has no pre-defined goal or target. One doesn't become "perfect" only better adjusted to the particular environment. This is why even highly evolved creatures such as humans are far from perfect. For example: the light sensitive cells in our eyes are mounted inside out[51], our spine is off center, and the birth canal is directly in between two major bones[52] et cetera.

The blindness of the process is sometimes challenged by people who suggest that the chance of a human evolving in a blind process would almost be zero, hence it didn't take place. This is statistically incorrect. Here is a small experiment: go to the nearest highway and write down the license plate number of the very first car that passes by, and then return home. The chance that you return with a license plate (any license plate) number is 100%. Now calculate the odds that out of all the cars in the world you happened to pick just that one license plate. That chance is almost zero. And yet you did it without difficulty. So the mere fact that doing it <u>again</u> seems impossible doesn't mean it didn't happen the <u>first time</u>.

In 1989 Dewdney[53] described a program in which tiny creatures called Flibs lived in an artificial world, and were subjected to evolution. The evolutionary mechanism used

---

[50] Hanberger H, cs. Low antibiotic resistance rates in Staphylococcus aureus, Escherichia coli and Klebsiella spp but not in Enterobacter spp and Pseudomonas aeruginosa: a prospective observational study in 14 Swedish ICUs over a 5-year period, Acta Anaesthesiol Scand. 2007 Aug;51(7):937-41

[51] Betancourt cs, Coherently radiating periodic structures (CORPS): a step towards high resolution imaging systems? Ant. and Prop. Soc. Int. Symp., 3-8 July 2005, 347- 350 vol. 4B ISBN: 0-7803-8883-6

[52] Karen Rosenberg, Wenda Trevathan, Birth, obstetrics and human evolution, An International Journal of Obstetrics and Gynaecology, Volume 109, Issue 11: 1199-1206.

[53] AK Dewdney, Scientific American, May 1989, based on an original design by Michael Palmiter, in line with Dawkin's "The blind watchmaker".

showed great similarity with the one described in the Blind Watchmaker[54]. Every creature has a set of genes that determine its behavior. Certain behavior results in finding food, other behavior doesn't. If a creature has eaten sufficient food it may reproduce, which means it may split itself into two creatures. One of these creatures is an exact copy, the other one gets a small change in its genes (a mutation). Eventually the group of creatures is perfectly adapted to the environment!

6.1   Breeding a robot

Based on that principle we will breed a robot, or rather its behavior. Our goal is to breed a robot that will stay within an area marked by a thick black line. What the robot does inside that area is irrelevant, as long as it never crosses the border. To avoid having to put together hundreds of robots we will start with a simulation on the PC. We will then turn the best-simulated robot behavior into a JAL program for a real robot.

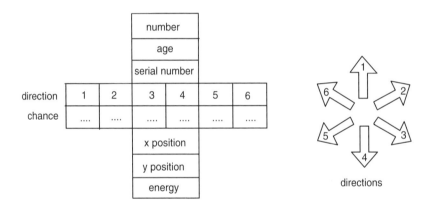

Figure 41. The robot genes.

The robots will get a set of genes[55] that determine their behavior, as shown in the previous Figure. The genes in this case consist of the chance to move in a certain direction.

[54] The Blind Watchmaker: Why the Evidence of Evolution Reveals a Universe Without Design by Richard Dawkins, 1986

[55] Based on an idea by Kees Vuik, Vuiks verhandelingen over computers, wetenschapen en denken, page 230-235, PCM/Prisma, 1992, ISBN902743123x ("Vuiks essays on Computers, Science and Thinking" published in Dutch only).

Direction

Possible directions in which the robot can move. A direction consists of a turn and a step forward. The turns are relative to the current direction. Direction 1 for example means go straight ahead. Whenever a robot hits a black area it will make a new decision regarding its direction.

Chance

This is the chance that a particular direction is selected. Directions with a higher chance are statistically selected more often. The choice is made using the roulette wheel mechanism as described in chapter 4.

Next to the genes other data is recorded for each robot. The most important one is age.

Age

Age of the robot, measured in the number of runs that the robot has survived. The most successful robot is therefor the robot with the highest age. So a measure for the success of the genes in the age of the robot that carries those genes. In Darwin's terms the age represents the "fitness" of this robot for this environment. There is no maximum age, and the behavior if the robot is not influenced by age.

A second important variable is the amount of energy that a robot has accumulated by eating food.

Energy

At each "step" that the robot takes energy is consumed. The energy supply can be replenished by finding food. In the simulation the food is colored black and yellow, and can only be found in particular locations in the virtual world. Any robot that wanders outside the food locations doesn't get anything to eat. When the energy runs out the robot dies and is removed from the simulation.

If a robot has gathered sufficient energy it is allowed to reproduce, or rather split (agamous reproduction). An exact copy is made, but in the new robot one of the direction chances receives a tiny change. Biologists would call this tiny change a mutation. The energy of the parent is split evenly between the parent and the child. The new robot gets a random location in the simulation.

It is this small mutation that drives the evolution. If it doesn't make the robot more successful in this environment the robot will die and the mutation will disappear. But if the mutation results in a better adapted robot (and thus a higher fitness, or age) chances are that this mutation is carried over to it's offspring. So successful mutations have a high chance of being sustained.

This is evolution in a nutshell. Without these small mutations the robots would never evolve, and thus never become non-linecrossers. This is not at all far fetched. Besides Darwin's theory there are numerous real life examples[56] of evolution in progress mainly in bacteria other pathogens, as well as insects. This simulation assumes by the way that behavior is hereditary, which in this case is of course correct, because we have programmed our robots that way.

The longer the simulation runs, the better the results. We are of course referring to the results for the group, or rather the species. In evolution the individual is of no importance.

The robot evolution simulation is a Visual Basic program. It is part of the download package. Once started you can adapt a whole range of settings. For your first experiments I would suggest to go with the default settings and simply click on "Start". Immediately the screen is filled with robots moving about.

Figure 42. The robot looks like a beetle..

If you look closely you see that the robots (the tiny creatures in the "Simulation" window") pretty much look like beetles. This is correct. The very first version of this program[57] was made in 1993 at which time I didn't have robots, but was training beetles instead.

After each run the statistics and the graph are updated. The "Best so far (red robot)" section is perhaps the most interesting one. This shows the genes of the most successful robot so far, and thus the evolutionary progress. The gene content in the screen print shown in the next Figure shows "0 0 5 20 20 5", which means this:

---

[56] Handel cs, The role of compensatory mutations in the emergence of drug resistance. PLoS Comput Biol. 2006 Oct;2(10):e137.
How does cross-reactive stimulation affect the longevity of CD8+ T cell memory? PLoS Comput Biol. 2006 Jun 9;2(6):e55. Epub 2006 Jun 9. Erratum in: PLoS Comput Biol. 2006 Jul 21:2(7):e97.
[57] Van Dam, January 1993, in Quick Basic 4.5.

straight ahead	60 degrees to the right	120 degrees to the right	reverse	120 degrees to the left	60 degrees to the left
0	0	5	20	20	5

As soon as this robot encounters a black area it will most likely reverse or turn 120 degrees to the left. How successful this strategy is in the long run remains to be seen, but so far it allowed him to survive for some 1674 runs and to get 82 offspring[58].

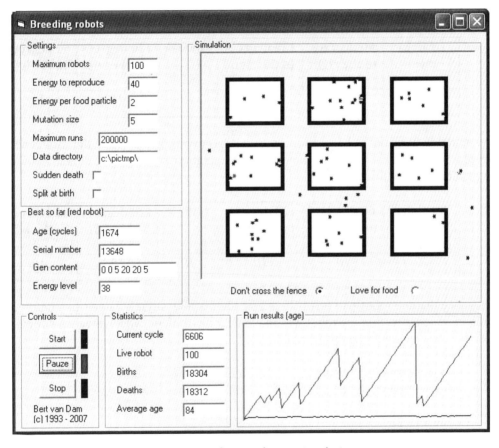

Figure 43. Robot evolution simulation.

---

[58] With the current settings moving one step yields two energy points. The first split takes place at energy level 40, which is then halved. So for subsequent splits only 20 additional energy points are required. That means there are $(1674-40)/20 + 1 = 82$ offspring.

Software

The first step in the mutation process is to determine whether the mutation will be up or down, meaning that a particular chance will be increased or decreased. That chance is 50/50.

The next step is to select a random gene. Then the mutation is carried out on that gene, with the restriction that the chance can never be smaller than zero.

If the robot has just started this will be its genes:

straight ahead	60 degrees to the right	120 degrees to the right	reverse	120 degrees to the left	60 degrees to the left
10	10	10	10	10	10

If the mutation turns out to be an addition, and it has to be carried out on the fifth gene the new genes would look like this (note that the mutation size is 5 by default, you can change that in the settings section):

straight ahead	60 degrees to the right	120 degrees to the right	reverse	120 degrees to the left	60 degrees to the left
10	10	10	10	15	10

The chance that the robot will turn 120 degrees left is now slightly larger than before. To decide in which direction the robot will move next the roulette wheel mechanism will be used. Which is handled like this in JAL:

```
-- select a random number from the roulette wheel
wheel=(random_byte*(gen1+gen2+gen3+gen4+gen5+gen6))/255

-- see in which action this number results
sel = 0
if wheel>0 & wheel<= gen1 then sel =  end if
if sel==0&wheel<= (gen1+gen2) then sel = 2 end if
if sel==0&wheel<= (gen1+gen2+gen3) then sel = 3 end if
if sel==0&wheel <= (gen1+gen2+gen3+gen4) then sel = 4 end if
if sel==0&wheel<=(gen1+gen2+gen3+gen4+gen5) then sel =5 end if
if sel==0 then sel=6 end if
```

Hardware

The sensor that is used to detect the black line consists of an infrared LED to illuminate the area and an infrared phototransistor to detect the reflected light. The sensor must be mounted between the wheels of the robot, exactly on the point of rotation. This will prevent the sensor from accidentally being moved to the other side of the black line simply because the robot is turning. The sensor used in this project is the QRB1134 infrared photo reflector, which has an LED, and phototransistor built in one package.

Figure 44. De QRB1134 mounted underneath the robot.

Figure 45. Electronics of the robot.

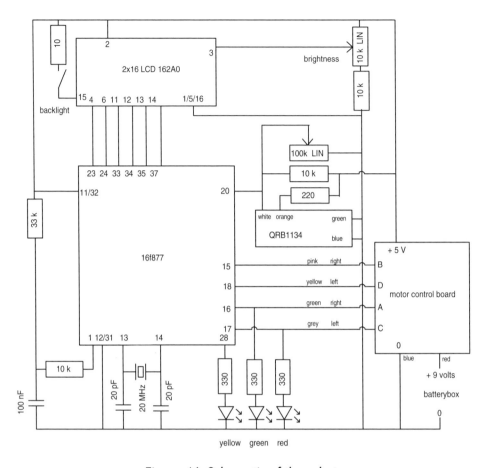

Figure 46. Schematic of the robot.

The Fairchild photo reflector is connected to pin 20. If you use a different sensor please note that the green/orange connections in the schematic are for the infrared LED, and the white/blue connections are for the phototransistor. In that case you may also need to use different resistors and a different variable resistor.

Once the robot has been built download this program into the robot:

> *-- JAL 2.3*
> include 16f877_bert

```
-- define the pins
pin_c0_direction = output        -- motor 1 (left side)
pin_c1_direction = output        -- motor 1 (left side)
pin_c2_direction = output        -- motor 2 (right side)
pin_c3_direction = output        -- motor 2 (right side)
pin_d1_direction = input         -- infrared reflector
pin_d5_direction = output        -- led yellow

-- brake the motors
pin_c1 = 0
pin_c2 = 0
pin_c3 = 0
pin_c4 = 0

forever loop

    -- LED on = black detected
    pin_d5 = pin_d1

end loop
```

Use the 100k variable resistor to fine adjust the sensor to distinguish between white and black, using a piece of black and white paper. The yellow LED should only be on when the sensor is on top of a black area.

Instructions

The PC program requires three files with the extension .DAT that must be in the data directory. If you use the default setting c:\picai\tmp\ and you installed the software exactly according to the instructions these files are automatically in the proper location.

You can use this program to breed two different types of robots. The choice is made using the radio buttons underneath the simulation window.

Don't cross the fence

This is the robot that is discussed in the section. The aim is to breed a robot that doesn't cross a black line (a "fence"). The yellow areas are enclosed with a black fence. Whenever the robot reaches the fence it makes a new decision as to which direction it will select next. In all other situation (both in the yellow and the white areas) it will move in a straight line.

Love for food

This is an alternative training. The goal is to train a robot to stay near a light source. The yellow food areas represent the light from such a light source. This time the robot takes a new decision about his direction at every step it takes.

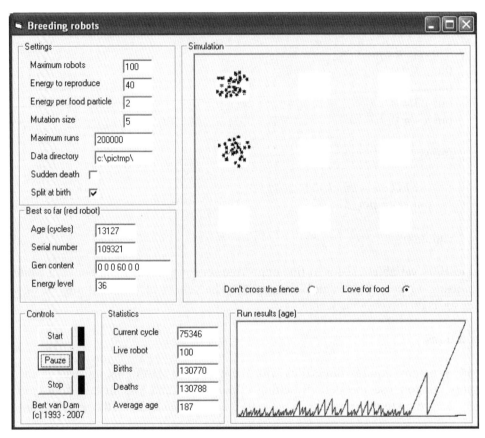

Figure 47. "Love for food".

In the previous picture "love for food" has been running for quite some time (about 75.000 runs). The best robot is very successful and has been alive for over 13.000 runs. His genes are "0 0 0 60 0 0", which means this:

straight ahead	60 degrees to the right	120 degrees to the right	reverse	120 degrees to the left	60 degrees to the left
0	*0*	*0*	*60*	*0*	*0*

This means it continuously takes a step forward and backward, effectively almost staying in the same location. Not very exciting to look at but, highly effective!

You can use this program by clicking "Start". With a lot of patience (it can easily take hours!) you can watch evolution in progress. There is of course no guarantee that the evolution reaches an (in your eyes) useful result. It is an unstructured blind process with unpredictable results. Once the preset number of runs is reached (or when you press "Stop") the program stops and writes a JAL program based on the best robot so far. The program is placed in the data directory. You open it in JALedit and then compile and download it into your robot in the usual manner.

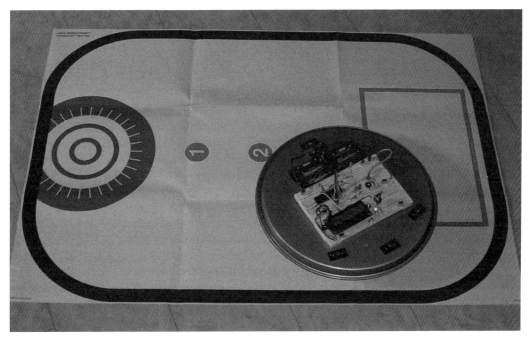

Figure 48. The "best robot so far" in action[59].

When you have your JAL program tape white paper on the floor and mark the boundaries with a thick black line (using a marker or black tape[60]). Put the robot in the middle of the area and switch it on. Without letting the wheels touch the ground hold it closely above the black line and check whether the yellow LED comes on to indicate that the black line has been detected. If this is not the case repeat the calibration process described earlier.

---

[59] The robot moves on a RoboSports™ Test Pad from a LEGO© Mindstorms™ kit. The blue and red lines and signs have no function in this situation..

[60] Please note that not all black tape is opaque to infra-red, so just because it looks black to you doesn't mean the sensor can see it!

If this works correctly put the robot down in the middle of the area and observe the result of the evolutionary breeding process.

Optional 1

You can change the settings of the program and see how that affects the end result.

Sudden death

> This means that robots will die as soon as they leave the food area.

Split at birth

> When a robot reproduces (splits) its offspring is placed at a random location in the simulation area. Using this option however the child will start its life at the exact same location as the parent. This is beneficial if the parent has obtained a "good" location and wishes his child to inherit this location.

Energy to reproduce

> This is the amount of energy required for a robot in order to reproduce. The higher this number the longer it takes before reproduction can take place. After reproduction both parent and child each receive half of that energy.

Energy per food particle

> The amount of energy a robot gets when it "eats" one bite (in reality when it moves one position in the feeding zone). Food is yellow and black, which means that robots are allowed to move continuously on top of the black line.

Mutation size

> During each split a small change is made in one of the direction chances of the offspring, the mutation. This variable indicates how large a mutation is.

Data directory

> In this directory (remember the slash at the end!) the log file resides, and the completed JAL program. The simulation program expects it's .DAT files in that directory also. Make sure that these .DAT files are in that directory before the program starts.

Optional 2

If you are an experienced Visual Basic programmer you can modify the simulation program (the sources are included in the download package). This allows you to breed robots for many other applications.

You could for example breed a line following robot. Perhaps the most logical setup consists of two sensors underneath the robot with the black line in between. But it can also be done using a single sensor that has to stay on top of the black line.[61]

With a bit more modifications you could breed a maze-solving robot. The maze could exist of black lines on the floor (hint: use two sensors on the periphery of the robot to stay between the lines) or a real maze with walls (hint: use ultrasonic sensors)[62].

Optional 3

In the data file *torstart.dat* the starting locations and starting genes of all robots are listed:

```
1 2 3  4   5   6   7   8   9   10   11   12
1, 1, 0, 10, 10, 10, 10, 10, 10, 500, 200, 10
1, 2, 0, 10, 10, 10, 10, 10, 10, 400, 300, 10
1, 3, 0, 10, 10, 10, 10, 10, 10, 300, 200, 10
1, 4, 0, 10, 10, 10, 10, 10, 10, 200, 100, 10
1, 5, 0, 10, 10, 10, 10, 10, 10, 100, 200, 10
1, 6, 0, 10, 10, 10, 10, 10, 10, 200, 300, 10
1, 1, 0, 10, 10, 10, 10, 10, 10, 300, 200, 10
1, 2, 0, 10, 10, 10, 10, 10, 10, 400, 100, 10
1, 3, 0, 10, 10, 10, 10, 10, 10, 500, 200, 10
1, 4, 0, 10, 10, 10, 10, 10, 10, 600, 300, 10
```

This is the content of this file (see also figure 41):

1	age	2	direction
3	serial number[63]	4	chance to move straight ahead

---

[61] Hint: you should let the robot follow the edge of the black line, so the sensor sees "grey". Depending on the change of color underneath the sensor (to either black or white) you know which way to turn the robot. This does mean that you must read the sensor using an analog input!

[62] Best known is the "left hand against the wall" method. If you start at an entrance and you keep your left hand against the wall at all times you will always find an exit (though not necessarily the one you had in mind).

5	chance to turn 60 degrees to the right	6	chance to turn 120 degrees to the right
7	chance to turn 180 degrees	8	chance to turn 60 degrees to the left
9	chance to turn 120 degrees to the right	10	X position
11	Y position	12	energy

You can open this file with Windows Notepad, and change the settings. It is perhaps a good idea to make a backup copy of this file first.

6.2   Wildebeest simulation

If you want to look for lions in Africa it's best to do this very early in the morning, shortly after dawn. Lions also hunt at night but then it is dark so you wouldn't see any of it. Search for a herd of wildebeest (or other prey) that appears to be staring at a single point. That single point is where the lions are. Since lions can run with more or less the same speed as wildebeest (both about 75 km/hr) the wildebeest are safe as long as they can see the lions and keep a sufficiently large distance. Lions are aware of this and mainly hunt by hiding and trying to surprise a wildebeest. As soon as a wildebeest spots a lion close by he starts running, thus alerting the entire herd. If the lion is close enough and fast enough it will get the wildebeest and eat it.

At the moment that the wildebeest starts running he is the closest animal to the lion. And he will remain in that position because the entire herd is alerted by him and starts running too. So if there is a victim, it's likely to be him.

That raises an interesting question. Wouldn't it be better for the wildebeest to pretend he didn't see the lion, and inconspicuously walk to the center of the herd to get as many animals between him and the lion?

To answer this question a simple PC simulation program will suffice. At the start of the program the wildebeest have one of three possible reactions when spotting a lion:

1.   Flee immediately ("alarm").
2.   Inconspicuously walk to the center of the herd ("walk").
3.   Ignore the lion ("ignore").

If a wildebeest has been devoured by a lion it will be replaced by a copy of the longest living wildebeest at that moment. This way the behavior of the herd can evolve to the most profitable behavior for an individual.

---

[63] The serial number is determined by the simulation program, always use 0.

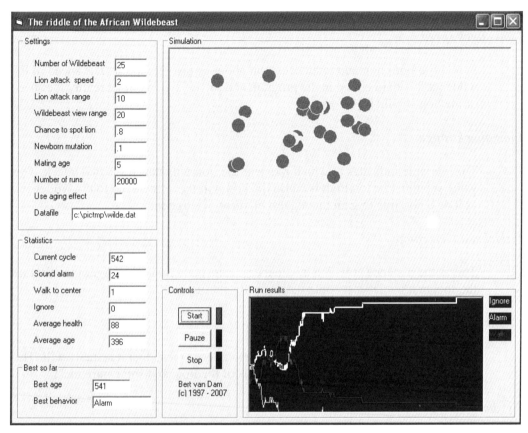

Figure 49. The riddle of the wildebeest.

In the download package you will find a simulation program for the PC. Press start without making any changes to the settings. In the simulation window the brown circles represent the wildebeest, grazing in a herd. They will move back and forth a bit while grazing, but they will stay close together. The yellow circle is the lion. He will sneak closer to the nearest wildebeest. If this wildebeest spots the lion it will behave as programmed in his genes. If that means running, than that will alert the entire herd, which will start running too. Wildebeest will move away from the lion, which may mean that the herd is split in two during the hunting process. Wildebeest are safe if they manage to leave the simulation windows. If all wildebeest have escaped, or one has been eaten, the statistics will be updated and the simulation will restart.

The graph shows the evolutionary results. In this case "Running" (white line) proves the most successful strategy indeed. Exactly as in real life. In most runs you will get this result.

The evolutionary results depend on a whole range of variable that can be adjusted freely:

Lion attack speed

In real life both lion and wildebeest run about as fast: 75 km/hr. The speed of the wildebeest is hard coded in the program and set at "2". To mimic reality the speed of the lion should be "2" too.

Lion attack range

This variable indicates at which moment the lion will start it's actual attack. This value shouldn't be too high because the lion will try to sneak up to the wildebeest as long a possible to gain the highest element of surprise.

Wildebeest view range

This is the distance at which a wildebeest can spot a lion. The larger this distance the sooner a wildebeest could theoretically start to run.

Chance to spot lion

The fact that a wildebeest could spot a lion doesn't mean that it actually will. This depends on the terrain, the sneaking skills of the lion, and some pure luck.

Newborn mutation

In some cases a newborn wildebeest will not be a copy of the longest living wildebeest, but it will have a mutation which causes a different behavior. If this behavior is advantageous it could take over the herd again. In a herd of runners inconspicuously walking might be an excellent survival strategy.

Mating age

The age at which wildebeest can mate. In reality this is irrelevant, and in this simulation too.

Use aging effect

If you select this option wildebeest will not live forever, but eventually die of old age. That means even a wildebeest with a highly successful survival strategy will eventually die.

The next graph shows a setting where inconspicuously walking to the center of the herd is indeed successful. The main difference in setting is that the wildebeest can't look very far (perhaps because it is dark, or the terrain contains excellent hiding places for the lion) combined with a lion that doesn't attack until the last minute.

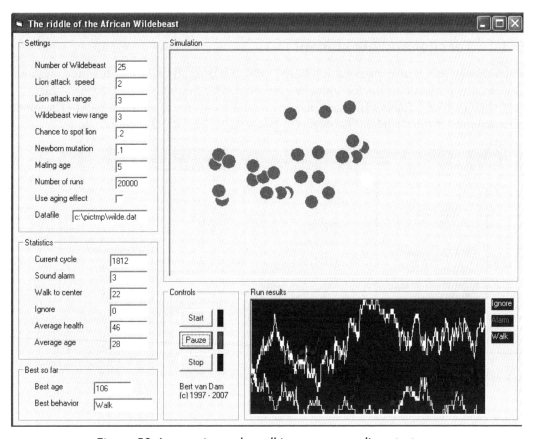

Figure 50. Inconspicuously walking away as ruling strategy.

Which strategy is the most successful depends on the circumstances. If we mimic reality as good as we can the "flee immediately" response is the most successful one, just like in real life. So even if other strategies did exist they have been eliminated over time by evolution as ruling strategy.

Optional 1

Apart from changing the settings experienced Visual Basic programmers could add different survival strategies to the program to see if they can change the course of evolution.

Optional 2

A certain setting will result in an oscillation between the three behaviors much like the case of the Uta Stansburiana as described in section 2.1. Perhaps this is the setting that most represents the actual situation.

6.3   Teacher and his student

Even though this is also an evolution-based project it is totally different than the previous two. In this project two microcontrollers are used. The first one (the "teacher") selects a sequence of four numbers (integers in the range 1 to 4), for example 1-3-2-4. The other microcontroller (the "student") now has to guess what the correct sequence is.

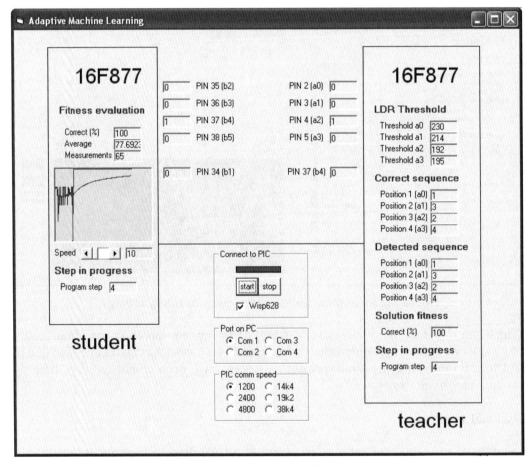

Figure 51. The teacher and his student. .

The teacher is connected to the PC and can relay information regarding it's own status as well as that from the student. On the PC a Visual Basic program is used to visualize the learning process. In the Figure below the student has guessed the teacher's sequence (1-3-2-4) in 44 tries, and after that answered correctly in 100% of the cases.

The process works like this: The teacher selects a sequence of four numbers. These numbers represent LEDs connected to the student. The sequence 1-3-2-4 for example means switch LED1 on momentarily, then LED3, then LED2 and then LED4. The sequence 1-1-1-1 for example means switch LED1 on momentarily, four times.

The student doesn't know which sequence the teacher has selected so he starts with a random sequence, for example 1-2-3-4. The teacher uses its LDRs to observe the sequence of the student. So the LED/LDR sets are an essential part in the learning process! Now the teacher calculates how many LEDs went on at the correct moment. If the teacher's sequence was 1-3-2-4 then two LEDs were correct:

	first LED	second LED	third LED	fourth LED
teacher	1	3	2	4
student	1	2	3	4
correct	x			x

So the fitness is two. This answer is relayed to the student, using a hardware RS232 connection between the two microcontrollers, and to the PC using a software serial RS232 connection. Please note that the student doesn't know which two LEDs are correct. This is basically a simplified game of Mastermind (which can by the way be solved in five steps or less[64]). If the answer was pulled from the student's brain (see the next paragraph) only the fitness needs to be stored. If the answer was adapted or new the student will first check if any solution currently in the brain has a lower, which means worse, fitness. If this is the case the sequence with the lower fitness will be replaced by the new sequence. The content of the brain is thus continually improving.

Now the student can try again. At first it checks his brain to see if it contains a correct sequence (so with fitness four). If this is the case it will show this sequence. If not it will in 90% of the cases pull an existing sequence from his brain, and in 90% of the cases make a small mutation in this sequence.

The new or made up sequence is executed using the LEDs and the cycle repeats itself.

---

[64] D. E. Knuth, "The computer as mastermind," Journal of Recreational Mathematics, Vol. 9, 1976, pp. 1-6.

The next Figure shows the program flow.

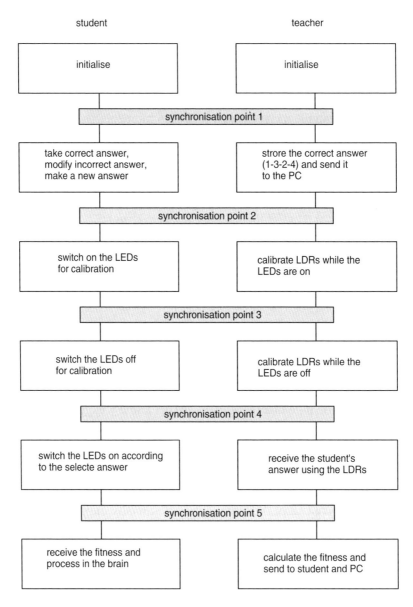

Figure 52. Flowchart of the teacher and his student.

The following two parts are noteworthy:

1. Even when a correct sequence is shown the fitness received from the teacher is stored in the brain.
2. Even when a sequence is pulled from the brain that is known to be incorrect (or rather: not completely correct) it is in 10% of the cases still shown to the teacher without any attempt of improvement.

These two deviations from logic are meant to keep the program flexible. If the teacher unexpectedly changes the correct sequence the student will respond immediately, even if it was convinced that the sequence it just showed was correct. It is a balance between finding a correct answer quickly and avoiding to get stuck in a local optimum.

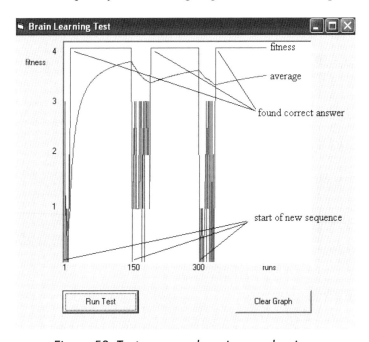

Figure 53. Test program learning mechanism.

The Figure above shows a Visual Basic version of the student brain learning mechanism. Each time that the correct sequence is changed the brain is taken off guard and gives the wrong answer. But immediately the learning mechanism kicks in and slowly the content of the brain is improving until suddenly the correct answer is discovered. From then on the student answers all questions correctly. Until of course the teacher changes the sequence, and the cycle starts all over again.

To further clarify this mechanism the following table shows the content of the student brain after the first question (n=1). The brain contains only one sequence, with a fitness of 2. That means that from this sequence two LEDs were lit at the correct moment. After ten questions (n=10) the brain is completely filled, and the best sequence has a fitness of three. After fifty questions (n=50) the correct answer has been found, with a fitness of four, obviously. After one hundred questions the content of the brain hasn't changed because once the correct answer is found the student uses that answer all the time.

n = 1
```
1>  1 2 1  1 fitness 2
2>            fitness 0
3>            fitness 0
4>            fitness 0
5>            fitness 0
```

n = 10
```
1>  1 2 1  4 fitness 3
2>  1 2 1  1 fitness 2
3>  1 2 1  3 fitness 2
4>  1 2 1  3 fitness 2
5>  1 3 1  2 fitness 1
```

n = 50
```
1>  1 2 3  4 fitness 4
2>  1 2 1  4 fitness 3
3>  1 2 1  4 fitness 3
4>  1 2 1  4 fitness 3
5>  1 2 1  4 fitness 3
```

n = 100
```
1>  1 2 3  4 fitness 4
2>  1 2 1  4 fitness 3
3>  1 2 1  4 fitness 3
4>  1 2 1  4 fitness 3
5>  1 2 1  4 fitness 3
```

It may have surprised you that this program is written in Visual Basic and runs on a PC, considering the fact that this is a test of the student brain, which is supposed to run in JAL in a microcontroller. In appendix 12.8 I will show you why I did this, and how easy it is to convert a Visual Basic source to JAL source.

The teacher and student programs must be completely in synch, otherwise the communication between them will falter. In the program sequence you may have spotted a series of synchronization points where the programs wait for each other. There are lots of different mechanisms available to achieve this, but the easiest is to use the buffers that belong to the hardware RS232 connection[65].

If a microcontroller receives a message over the hardware serial connection, but doesn't have time to process it yet, this message is stored in a buffer[66]. A program that reaches a synchronization point sends a message to the other microcontroller and waits for a reply. If the other microcontroller reached this point first the reply is received immediately (from the buffer!) and the program may continue. If the other microcontroller has not reached that point yet, the program simply waits for this to happen. When it does happen it will receive a reply (directly this time) and continue. A very simple and very effective technique.

This is an example of a synchronization point in the two programs listed next to each other[67].

Teacher	Student

mydata = "0"
Serial_HW_Write("B")
while mydata != "A" loop
   Serial_HW_Read(mydata)
end loop
	mydata = "0"
	  while mydata != "B" loop
	    Serial_HW_Read(mydata)
	  end loop
	  Serial_HW_Write("A")

If you take a look at the JAL sources you will notice that extensive calibration takes place both when the LEDs are on as well as when they are off. This is an automatic correction for changes in ambient light intensity. Without this you would manually have to calibrate them repeatedly. The variable resistors are for course calibration in case the automatic calibration is out of range. Normally this should not happen if the variable resistors are in mid position.

---

[65] Van Dam, PIC Microcontrollers, 50 projects for beginners and experts, Elektor ISBN 978-0-905705-70-5 page 254.
[66] Note that these buffers can only contain two bytes. In case you want to read the relevant section in the datasheet; the buffer is called *rcreg*
[67] The exclamation mark means "not". So != means: not equal to .

Hardware

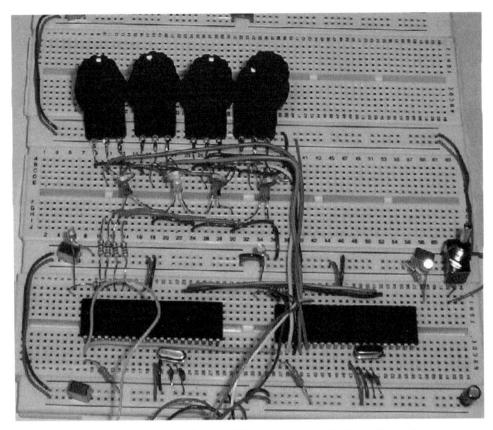

Figure 54. The teacher and his student on the breadboard.

The hardware can be built using the picture and the schematic. Make sure the LEDs and LDRs are mounted opposite from each other, and possibly against each other. The four variable resistors can be used for rough calibration. Otherwise too much ambient light will prevent auto calibration from working correctly.

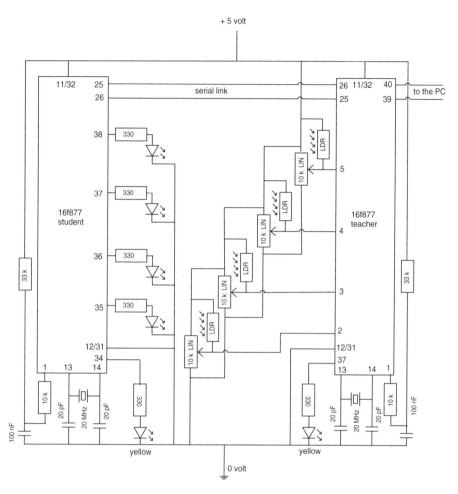

Figure 55. Schematic of the teacher and his student.

The teacher uses a software serial connection to communicate to the PC (using the Wisp programmer pass-through functionality) and a hardware serial connection to communicate information to the student. Note that the student can only reply using its LEDs.

Instructions

Avoid direct ambient light on the LDRs. The four variable resistors are approximately in mid position. Switch the power on and download the student program in the left microcontroller and the teacher program in the right microcontroller. Switch the power supply off, wait a moment, and the switch it back on. This way the programs start synchronized. Enjoy the learning student.

Optionally you can use the Visual Basic program on the PC to visualize the learning process. This is certainly worth while! Connect the Wisp programmer to the right microcontroller on the breadboard (the teacher). Connect the yellow programmer wire not just to the teacher, but also to the student (on pin 1), so to <u>both</u> microcontrollers at the same time and leave these wires connected[68]. Start the Visual Basic program. The microcontrollers will be restarted through the yellow wire and are automatically in synch.

Optional 1

Contrary to the teacher in the Visual Basic student brain test program the JAL teacher uses only one sequence. You could change the JAL program in the teacher to make it change the correct sequence at irregular intervals, and see how the student responds.

Optional 2

The way that the student uses its brain reflects my ideas on optimizing between speed and flexibility. You can change this mechanism and see if you agree with me, or that perhaps a different setting improves the learning process.

Optional 3

The sequence that the teacher comes up with has to contain exactly four numbers, with other words a (any) LED must momentarily be on four times. Is it possible to see an LED that doesn't flash as a valid part of the sequence? For example 1-0-2-3, where LED 1 goes on momentarily, then there is a short pause, and the LEDs two and three go on momentarily?

Optional 4

Currently the program uses a "blind evolutionary" mechanism. A human player would use the teacher's feedback to try to predict which LED was correct and which one was not. Is it possible to add this intelligence to this program?

---

[68] When the Wisp is switched to pass through mode it resets the connected microcontroller using pin 1. Since both microcontrollers must start in synch that means that the other one must be restarted also. The easiest way to achieve this is to connect both pin 1's to the Wisp (yellow wire).

7   Genetic algorithm

In the previous chapter a simple evolutionary algorithm was used which in nature occurs in simple creatures such as bacteria. More complex creatures (such as humans) use a more complex mechanism.

Instead of a simple split of the genes complex creatures get a part of their genes from each parent, and thus also a part of the hereditary characteristics. If the parents get more than one child then these children often inherit different characteristics. This means both parents do not hand down a fixed part of their genes to the next generation, but a changing part.

Which characteristics are hereditary is a constant source of discussion, often called the "nature versus nurture" controversy. Children within a single family can often grow up to very different adults, while identical twins split at birth, which grow up completely separated from each other, can often have a strikingly similar behavior. A lot of research has been done in this area, which unfortunately doesn't bring much clarification. Bateson's[69] summary gives a very good overview of this controversy

It is clear however that hereditary characteristics exist, so in 1975 Holland[70] translated the way that genes are transferred from parents to children into a computer model. Due to the apparent parallel with biological genetics he called his technique "genetic algorithm". Nowadays genetic algorithms are used in areas where more traditional problem solving techniques do not deliver sufficiently satisfying results[71].

How genetic algorithms work can best be explained using an example. Let us assume that we are looking from a number in the range 0 to 255, which has the larger possible square. The answer is of course 255, with square $255^2 = 65.025$, but let's pretend we do not know this. We start with two random numbers, for example 86 and 167 and note these in 8 bits binary[72]:

01010110 and 10100111

---

[69] Bateson, Patrick, Where does our behaviour come from?, J. Biosci., Vol. 26, No. 5, December 2001, 561–570

[70] John H. Holland, Adaptation in Natural and Artificial Systems, An Introductory Analysis with Applications to Biology, Control, and Artificial Intelligence, University of Michigan Press 1975 ISBN: 9780472084609

[71] Goldberg, David E, Genetic Algorithms in Search, Optimization and Machine Learning, Addison-Wesley Publishing company Inc, 1989, ISBN 0-201-15767-5

[72] On the internet you can find many useful calculators which allow you to convert between decimal and binary, such as calc98: www.calculator.org/download.html

These are the chromosomes of the parents, often just called "parents". We now select a random point, for example between the third and the fourth gene and cut both chromosomes in two parts. We then exchange the parts and put them back together crossed over.

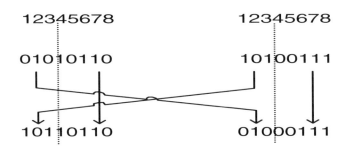

Figure 56. Chromosome crossover between gene 3 and 4.

This results in two new numbers, namely 10110110 and 01000111. These are the chromosomes of the children, often just called "the children". We now calculate the fitness of both parents and children. In effect we calculate how well suited these chromosomes are in their environment. In this example the environment is "raise to a square", and being suited to this environment means "having a high squared value".

chromosome	number		fitness
	binary	decimal	(square)
parent 1	01010110	86	7396
parent 2	10100111	167	27.889
child 1	10110110	182	33.124
child 2	01000111	71	5041

The total population contains four chromosomes. We now select the two chromosomes that are best suited to their environment, which would be 10100111 and 10110110.

Normally speaking there would be many more chromosomes in a population, so determining who gets to cross over and with whom is less obvious. Genetic algorithms generally speaking use the roulette wheel mechanism as discussed in chapter four. If you have not read that chapter now would be a good time to do so.

For the previous table the roulette wheel would look like this:

Figure 57. Roulette wheel to select crossover.

If the fitness values are too far apart some chromosomes might be selected too often. By the same token: if the fitness values are too close together the distinguishing properties of fitness size would be lost. In those situations scaling is used. The scaling factor is an indication of how often the best chromosome will be selected (on average) over the worst chromosome. Values between 1 and 2 are normally used. The next Figure shows the effect of scaling on the roulette wheel.

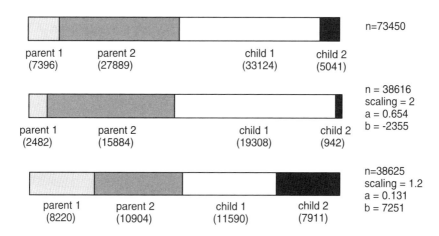

Figure 58. Scaling effect (none, 2 and 1.2).

It is possible that some chromosomes get to crossover (mate) more than once, and others never. This is completely in line with nature. A dominant male ape[73] for example will not limit itself to impregnating just the alpha female, but it will try to impregnate as many female apes as possible, preferably all females in the group. In humans for example some people have multiple children, while others have none.

[73] Pope, Theresa R, The reproductive consequences of male cooperation in the red howler monkey: paternity exclusion in multi-male and single-male troops using genetic markers, Behavioral Ecology and Sociobiology, Volume 27, Number 6 / December, 1990

The scaling formula[74] is $f_{scaled} = a * f_{oud} + b$

where

$$a = \frac{(scale-1) * f_{gem}}{f_{max} - f_{min}}$$

$$b = \frac{f_{gem} * (f_{max} - scale * f_{gem})}{f_{max} - f_{min}}$$

with $\quad f_{scaled}$ = fitness after scaling
$\quad\quad\quad f_{oud}$ = fitness before scaling
$\quad\quad\quad f_{max}$ = maximum fitness
$\quad\quad\quad f_{min}$ = minimum fitness
$\quad\quad\quad f_{gem}$ = average fitness

As an example we will convert the fitness of parent one in the previous figure (7396) to the scaled fitness f_{scaled} from the second line (2482) using a scaling factor of 2:

$$a = \frac{(scale-1) * f_{gem}}{f_{max} - f_{min}} = \frac{(2-1) * 18362}{33124 - 5041} = 0.654$$

and

$$b = \frac{f_{gem} * (f_{max} - scale * f_{gem})}{f_{max} - f_{min}} = \frac{18362 * (33124 - 2 * 18362)}{33124 - 5041} = -2354$$

which means that f_{scaled} is:

$$f_{scaled} = a * f_{oud} + b = 0.654 * 7396 - 2355 = 2482$$

Chromosomes that have been selected based on the fitness will by the way not necessarily perform an actual crossover, or in human terms: procreate. Just like in the real world they may not "like" each other, or even worse: they never actually "meet" each other at all. In calculations a crossover factor is used, in percentages usually about 85%.

In any given chromosome there can never be more "1" genes than originally present in the genetic material of the parents of that population. A genetic algorithm, based on the two parents in our simple example (86 and 167) will never achieve a higher fitness than

---

[74] Goldberg, David E, Genetic Algorithms in Search, Optimization and Machine Learning, Addison-Wesley Publishing company Inc, 1989, ISBN 0-201-15767-5

61.009 (the square of 11110111), because none of the parents has a "1" for the 5th gene. This is called a local maximum or optimum.

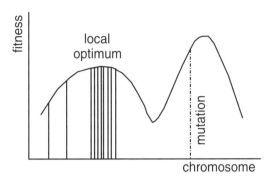

Figure 59. Escaping the local optimum.

To prevent this from happening first of all the population should be much larger. Several hundreds of parents is very normal. Secondly the driving force behind evolution needs to be used: mutation. .Mutation is a small random change in a gene (one of the positions in a chromosome).

Mutation is a very common mechanism in nature. When the environment changes and a new optimum is possible mutation will enable the species to escape into this new optimum. An example would be bacteria gaining resistance against antibiotics[75]. In the changed environment (which now contains antibiotics) bacteria with some resistance will achieve a better fitness[76], namely staying alive longer. Surviving more generations means producing more offspring, which means this new mutation will quickly gain a foothold. Usually a low value is used for the mutation rate, or chance of a mutation: 5% or less.

---

[75] Bruce R. Levin, Compensatory Mutations, Antibiotic Resistance and the Population Genetics of Adaptive Evolution in Bacteria, Genetics, Vol. 154, 985-997, March 2000
[76] J. L. Martinez, Mutation Frequencies and Antibiotic Resistance, Antimicrobial agents and chemotherapy, July 2000, p. 1771–1777 44, No. 7

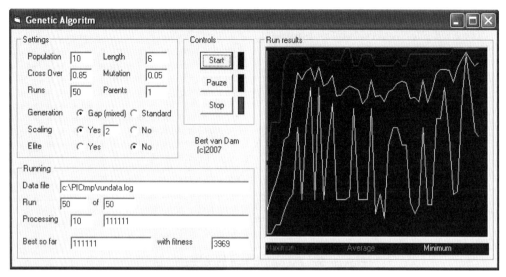

Figure 60. Genetic algorithm in search of a high squared value.

In the download package you will find a program to find the highest squared value, just like in the example we started manually. Since you already know what the correct answer is you can use this program to get a feel for the different variables and the impact that they have on the genetic algorithm.

The program uses three inter-connected arrays. The base array is the "population" array. Using the roulette wheel mechanism chromosomes are selected from this array that may participate in the procreation process. It is possible that the same chromosomes are selected more than once. These chromosomes are copied to the "parent" array.

Optionally you can select a completely random draw[77] instead of the roulette wheel mechanism for all or part of the selection process. In the "settings" section you can use the "parents" to indicate which part of the parents should be selected using the roulette wheel (1 = 100%).

From the parent array chromosomes are copied in groups of two for crossover (procreation). The result is stored in the "children" array. So in the children array only crossed-over chromosomes can be found. In theory anyway, because one of the settings is "cross-over". This is the chance that two chromosomes actually mate. If the answer is "no" the chromosomes do not crossover and are stored in the children array "as is".

---

[77] A completely random partner choice occurs for example in the case of plants that are pollinated by insects or the wind.

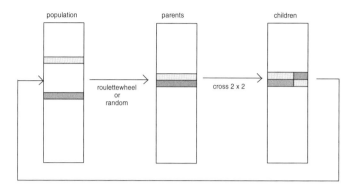

Figure 61. Genetic algorithm array relationship.

In the example at the beginning of this section you saw that we selected the best chromosomes from a mixed group of parents and children. This mixed group selection is called the "generation gap" model. If you select this model (select: "Generation: Gap") then out of every four parents two perform a cross over and two are copied "as is" as shown in the next Figure.

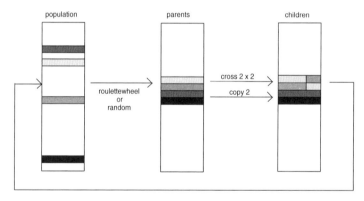

Figure 62. The same, but now with generation gap enabled.

The variables that have not been discussed yet are:

Variable	Description
Population	The number of chromosomes to be used. This has to be an even number to allow pair-wise cross over.
Length	The number of genes in the chromosome (in this case the number of bits).
Elite	It is possible that a very good solution gets lost in time because the particular chromosome is not selected for mating. An "unpopular" chromosome so to speak. By enabling this variable ("yes") you force the genetic algorithm to carry the best chromosome over to the next generation.

All data of the genetic algorithm is stored in a data file. Per run and per chromosome the fitness is listed. In the last column the percentile fitness of the chromosome is shown. At the end of each run the mutations are listed. Do check out the data file because it contains a lot of interesting information about the way that this exciting mechanism works.

Run 3 of 50

1	101000	1600	8
2	110000	2304	11
3	101000	1600	8
4	101101	2025	10
5	110000	2304	11
6	101101	2025	10
7	101101	2025	10
8	110000	2304	11
9	110000	2304	11
10	100001	1089	5

Fitness statistics: Avg = 1958 Max = 2304 Min = 1089

Mutation 101101   101001
Mutation 110000   100000

All genetic algorithm programs in this book show a graph containing minimum, maximum and average value. This is of course fun to watch, but it is also an important way to spot if different settings may need to be used. The most important determining value for this is the spread, or rather the relative spread (spread in relation of the mean value):

$$\text{spread percentage} \quad = \quad \frac{\text{maximum - minimum}}{\text{mean}} \qquad (\text{in \%})$$

If the spread percentage is too small the population contains too little statistically different genetic material to achieve a serious improvement of the fitness. If that happens when the fitness is still low in your opinion you may want to retry this run, or modify the settings (and then restart). At the end of a series of runs it is normal for the spread to deteriorate: this means the genetic algorithm has reached it's local optimum.

In the minimum fitness serious downward spikes are normal: these are almost always mutations that didn't work out too well for the individual concerned.

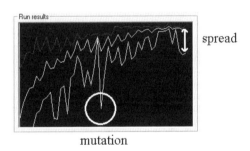

mutation

Figure 63. Spread and mutation spikes.

In order to use a genetic algorithm to solve a real life problem you need to take the following six steps:

1. Translate the question to a chromosome.
2. Design a method to automatically determine the fitness of a chromosome.
3. Generate a sufficiently large random population.
4. Select chromosomes and perform a crossover.
5. Occasionally mutate.
6. Check to see if the fitness is high enough to stop, or if sufficient runs have been made. If no go back to step 4.

The first step is usually the most difficult. It must be possible to cut a chromosome at a random location, perform a crossover with a completely different chromosome, and still end up with a valid chromosome.

7.1   The longest distance

Time to put our genetic algorithm knowledge into practice. In this project we will breed a program that makes a robot drive the longest distance. We assume that there are no obstacles, and that the only question is how efficient the genetic algorithm can be in a simple robot application.

In order to breed a program it must be treated by a genetic algorithm as a chromosome. That means it should be built in such a way that the cross-over mechanism can cut it into half, put it back crossed over, and still end up with a valid program. That means we need to find a "robot chromosome". A convenient way is to model robotic behavior in behavioral blocks. Each of these blocks represents a typical robot behavior, for example "make a turn". These blocks can be put together in any order, and still yield a working program. A mutation could mean changing one block into another. Biologically speaking a block is the equivalent of a gene.

Block	Description
B00	Stand still.
B01(x)	Move x centimeters straight ahead.
B02	Turn 360 degrees.
B03(x)	Turn x degrees to the right.
B04(x)	Turn x degrees to the left.
B05(x)	Move x centimeters to a light spot.
B06(x)	Move x centimeters to a dark spot.
B07(x)	Move x centimeters backwards.

The blocks B05 and B06 first make the robot turn 360 degrees to determine the proper direction to a light or dark spot. Then the robot turns back to that particular direction and moves forward x centimeters. So this program will make the robot determine where the light source is and drive 35 cm toward it[78]:

    B05(35)

---

[78] One inch is 2.54 centimeters.

And with this program the robot will move in a square with 10 centimeter sides:

B01(10) B3(90) B01(10) B3(90) B01(10) B3(90) B01(10)

If you read ahead in this section you may have noticed that the genetic algorithms do not use the block for reverse. Since most of the sensors are at the front of the robot the preferred direction is forward. Instead of backing up the sequence B03(180)B01(x) would be safer.

A real life JAL program might look like this:

```
-- JAL 2.3
include 16f877_bert
include robot_bert

B05(10)
B03(45)
B06(10)
B05(10)
B06(10)
B05(10)
B01(10)
B05(10)
B05(10)
B02
B06(10)
B06(10)
```

In fact this is a real JAL program, bred by the "In search of light" project fo section 7.2. The listing of blocks in this program is actually a series of calls to procedures in the robot_bert library. You will find this library in the library directory in the download package. Since different robots will have different driving and turning speeds the library needs calibration data.

```
-- robot motor dependent times in mS
fwd_1_cm = 10
rght_1_deg = 81
lft_1_deg = 78
```

These data represent how long it takes (in milliseconds) for your robot to move one centimeter forward (*fwd_1_cm*), turn one degree to the right (*rght_1_deg*) or to the left (*lft_1_deg*). While building the robot according to the instructions in the appendix a program was shown to test the robot. You can use this program to measure how much the robot moves in a certain time and convert that to the data required for calibration. Don't worry too much about accuracy. If you want to be accurate you need to use wheel sensors for reliable movement detection. None of the projects in this book require that kind of accuracy.

This is an example of the B03 procedure that lets the robot turn "degr" degrees to the right using the calibration data:

```
procedure B03 (byte in degr) is
    -- turn right degr degrees
    pin_c0 = 1
    pin_c1 = 0
    pin_c2 = 1
    pin_c3 = 0
    for degr loop
        delay_1ms(rght_1_deg)
    end loop
    pin_c0 = 0
    pin_c1 = 0
    pin_c2 = 0
    pin_c3 = 0
end procedure
```

Note that behavior block B00 (stand still) does exist in the library, but it is never used in the genetic algorithm programs. You might try using it in the next project and see what happens.

It is rather inconvenient that block names such as B01(x) and B02 do not have the same length. If we line these two blocks up and cut this chromosome in the middle we will have cut halfway through one of the blocks. For that reason we will normalize all behaviors to standard values for x. For movement we chose $x = 10$ and for turning we chose $x = 45$. So if the genetic algorithm refers to gene B03 it actually means block B03(45). *So a chromosome does not contain length and angle instructions but a behavior block does.* You can by the way use blocks for other purposes as well: this is a really easy way to write a robot program!

Software

The aim of this project is for the robot to cover as large a distance as possible. We will define distance as down range, not the shortest line between start and end of the trajectory. Determining the fitness of the robot chromosome is very simple because only blocks B01, B05 and B06 add to the traveled distance. In all other blocks the robot is not moving or just turning on the spot.

In the software download you will find a Visual Basic program for this genetic algorithm.

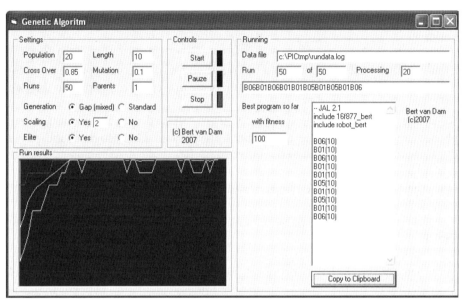

Figure 64. The longest distance.

The genetic algorithm correctly concludes that stacking B01, B05 and B06 blocks in the program as much as possible is the proper way to go. With ten genes the algorithm wrote a program that lets the robot move one meter, the maximum possible distance.

```
-- JAL 2.1
include 16f877_bert
include robot_bert

B06(10)
B01(10)
B06(10)
B01(10)
B01(10)
B05(10)
B01(10)
B05(10)
B01(10)
B06(10)
```

Hardware

As hardware you can use the robot from any of the other projects. It doesn't matter which project you chose because all you need are two motors, which every robot in this book is bound to have.

Instructions

The default settings of the program will do, but if you want you can change the settings to your liking. Instructions as to what these settings mean were given earlier in this section.

Wait for the genetic algorithm to finish. If you are satisfied with the result use the "copy to clipboard" button to copy the automatically generated JAL program and past it into JALedit. Compile and download to the microcontroller in the usual manner.

Make sure the robot has sufficient space (with the default settings one meter), and switch it on.

Optional 1

You can breed a different behavior by setting a different goal for the robot. Which goal that is, is determined by the fitness calculation. Fitness calculation happens in this section of the Visual Basic program:

```
For t = 1 To Len(behaviour$) Step 3
    test = Val(Mid$(behaviour$, t + 1, 3))
    Select Case test
        Case 0
        Case 1
            Fitness = Fitness + 10
        Case 2
        Case 3
        Case 4
        Case 5
            Fitness = Fitness + 10
        Case 6
            Fitness = Fitness + 10
    End Select
    ' other commands
Next t
```

The number following *Case* is the number of the gene. So B01 is *Case 1*, B05 is *Case 5* et cetera. You can use multiple statements per case if you want. A not very useful example:

```
Case 5
    Fitness = Fitness + 5
    Fitness = Fitness + 5
```

By changing the fitness rules you can for example breed a robot that has to travel the longest distance *in a straight line*.

Optional 2

You can also make combinations that only result in fitness when two genes are in the right order right behind each other. You can easily achieve this by remembering the value of *test* (which is the current gene number) by storing it in a variable called *lasttest*. When the next gene is processed compare *test* to *lasttest* to see if the genes are in the right order. For example like this:

```
For t = 1 To Len(behaviour$) Step 3
    lasttest = test
    test = Val(Mid$(behaviour$, t + 1, 3))
    Select Case test
        Case 0
        Case 1
            If lasttest = 3 Then Fitness = Fitness + 10
        Case 2
        Case 3
            If lasttest = 1 Then Fitness = Fitness + 10
        Case 4
        Case 5
        Case 6
    End Select
    ' other commands
Next t
```

This genetic algorithm now favors combinations of B01B03 and B03B01, as you can see in the next Figure.

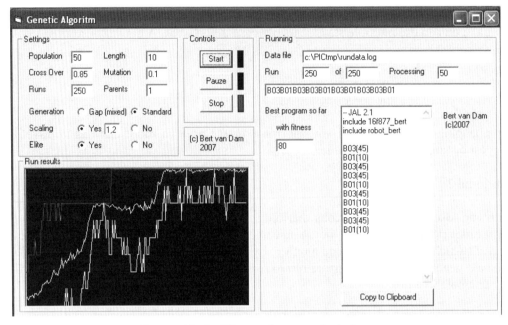

Figure 65. A different fitness calculation.

The results of a genetic algorithm may vary. A solution will be found which more or less satisfies the requirements, but it is still possible for the algorithm to be trapped in a local optimum. Sometimes the algorithm yields a surprisingly nice result. The algorithm described above bred this program in one of the runs!

```
-- JAL 2.1
include 16f877_bert
include robot_bert

B03(45)
B01(10)
B03(45)
B01(10)
B03(45)
B01(10)
B03(45)
B01(10)
B03(45)
B01(10)
```

Which is an exceptionally nice path.

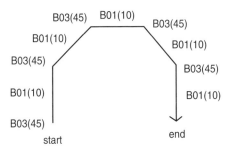

Figure 66. Genetic algorithm result.

Optional 3

It may be a good idea to add a piece of software to the robot that makes it avoid obstacles. A small hint is that it is probably best to adapt your version of robot_bert. You will need to add your modifications inside the waiting loops. If you have no clue how to do this perhaps you should wait until project 10.3 (the subsumption robot "The Hunter").

7.2   In search of light

In the previous project the goal was straightforward and so was the fitness calculation. That is about to change. In this project the robot has to search for a light source and stay near it as long as possible. Much like a robot looking for sunlight to recharge it's solar cells, or a lizard that wants to warm up in the sun. To keep the simulation visually interesting an added condition is that the robot must keep moving.

We could calculate the fitness with a mathematical formula, but performing an on-screen simulation would be much more fun. The genetic algorithm program used in this chapter is basically the same as in the previous chapter.

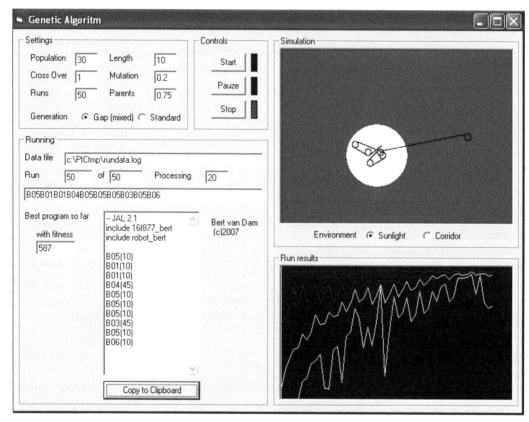

Figure 67. In search of light.

New is the simulation window in the top right corner. The black line is the path the robot has followed. This path is determined by the chromosome bred by the genetic algorithm. The circles represent the light source. The yellow circle is the light itself. The robot gets a reward if it moves within that circle. The white circle around it is sufficiently close to the light to get a reward too, but not as much. The rest of the room is too far away from the light and yields no reward. The fitness is determined according to the following table

color	fitness
yellow (center)	2 points per step
white (periphery)	1 point per step
remaining	no points

In the previous Figure the genetic algorithm has done an excellent job with this particular chromosome: a fitness of 587. After determining where the light source is located the robot moves straight towards it. After arrival it repeatedly uses B05 genes (B05(10) blocks) to stay within that area and make as many tight turns as it can. This is the generated program:

```
-- JAL 2.1
include 16f877_bert
include robot_bert

B05(10)
B01(10)
B01(10)
B04(45)
B05(10)
B05(10)
B05(10)
B03(45)
B05(10)
B06(10)
```

It is interesting to see that the program ends with a B06 gene, or search a dark spot. In real life everything outside the circles might be considered "dark" by the robot. In this simulation however a "dark spot" has been defined in the upper right corner of the simulation area. Since the robot path happens to end exactly at the other side of the light the B06(10) happens to move the robot underneath the light one final time, and pick up some extra fitness on the way.

In one of the earlier versions of this program one of the runs achieved an exceptionally good result. As it turned out this program didn't have one single B05 gene in it! The robot just happened to move in the right direction, and achieved a perfect fitness. It was not what I had anticipated, but the genetic algorithm did a perfect job: it bred a program that was perfectly adapted to the environment.

After that interesting experience the program, or rather the environment, has been changed. Now the light source is moved to a different location and a different distance from the starting point at every run. Only robots capable of efficiently searching for the light source can achieve good results. There are three different light source locations in use.

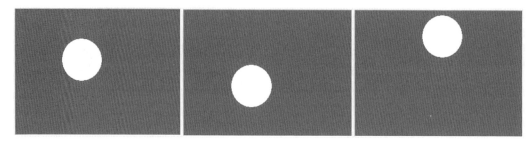

Figure 68. The three different light source locations.

This explains why the fitness graph will show a saw tooth pattern in the early runs. There will be no chromosome (yet) that is capable of performing well for all of the three light source locations.

Hardware

Figure 69. LDR on the front side of the robot.

The schematic and the picture of the breadboard can be used to build this project. Of course you need to build the robot itself, the motor control electronics and the battery pack as per the instructions in the appendix. New is the LDR that needs to be mounted on the front side of the robot.

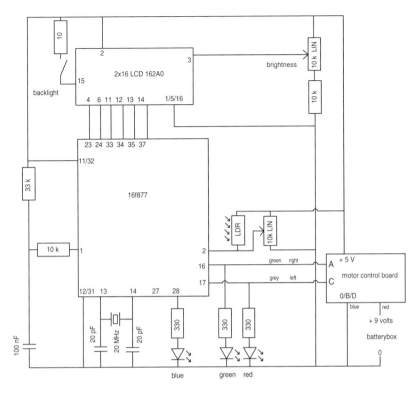

Figure 70. In search of light.

Instructions

You can run the program with the default settings (recommended for the first run) or modify the settings to your liking. The impact of these setting has been discussed earlier. The program will take a long time to complete. This is because all chromosomes are drawn in the simulation window at such a speed that you can actually see (and enjoy) it. One hour for an algorithm to complete is not uncommon, algorithms with a larger number of runs or more chromosomes may easily take many hours.

Once you are satisfied with the result use the "copy to clipboard" button to copy the program, and past it into JALedit. The program can be compiled and downloaded into the microcontroller in the usual manner.
Place the robot about 30 centimeters away from a lamp. The lamp should be on the right hand side of the robot, so it should not face the lamp!

Make sure the lamp is mounted very low, but leave enough clearance for the robot to move underneath it. A not too bright mains lamp with a dimmer switch is convenient. It is easier to change the settings of the dimmer than to recalibrate the robot. It will definitely take you some time to get the light intensity just right. Make sure the rest of the room is completely dark, and remove any obstacles from the robot area.

If your program contains one or more B06(x) blocks the result may deviate from the result of the on-screen simulation. In reality the entire surrounding of the robot area is dark, so acceptable for the B06 block. In the simulation however the dark spot is a well-defined area on the top right side of the simulation windows.

Local optimum

In the introduction to the genetic algorithm the risk was discussed that the algorithm could get stuck in a local optimum. Mutations are used to prevent this and explore other possibilities. This is an example of a real run that got stuck in a local optimum. From left to right each line contains the chromosome number, the chromosome itself, the fitness and the percentage that this fitness has of the total of this run.

1	B05B04B04B01B05B05B03B05B04B05	558	4
2	B02B04B04B01B05B05B04B04B04B05	370	0
3	B02B04B04B02B05B03B03B05B04B05	445	1
4	B05B04B04B01B05B05B04B05B04B05	585	4
5	B05B04B04B01B05B05B04B05B04B05	585	4
6	B05B04B04B02B05B05B04B05B04B05	806	9
7	B05B04B04B01B05B05B04B05B04B05	585	4
8	B05B04B04B02B05B05B04B05B04B05	806	9
9	B05B04B04B01B05B05B04B05B04B05	585	4
10	B02B04B04B02B05B03B03B05B04B05	445	1
11	B02B04B04B01B05B05B03B05B04B05	517	3
12	B02B04B04B02B05B03B04B05B04B05	450	1
13	B05B04B04B01B05B05B04B05B04B05	585	4
14	B05B04B04B01B05B05B04B05B04B05	585	4
15	B04B04B04B01B05B05B04B05B04B05	803	9
16	B05B04B01B01B05B05B04B05B04B05	825	10
17	B05B04B04B01B05B05B04B05B04B05	585	4
18	B05B04B04B01B05B05B04B05B04B05	585	4
19	B05B04B04B01B05B05B04B05B04B05	585	4
20	B05B04B04B01B05B05B04B05B04B05	585	4

In all chromosomes the second gene is B04.

That is rather unfortunate because B04 is a 45 degree turn to the right. The chromosome almost has to start with gene B05 to locate the light but invariably B04 will throw it off course so it ends next to the yellow area. The result is still quite acceptable (that is the power of the genetic algorithm) but it could be better if there was more gene diversity. Note that the next Figure is from an older version of the program where the light source was larger.

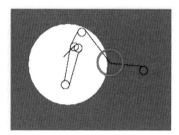

Figure 71. B04 as second gene causes a local optimum..

Optional 1

So far we have used the simulation to search for light. The program supports a second simulation possibility called corridor. You can select this simulation using the radio buttons below the simulation window. The corridor simulation consists of a "yellow corridor" in which the robot has to linger as long as possible.

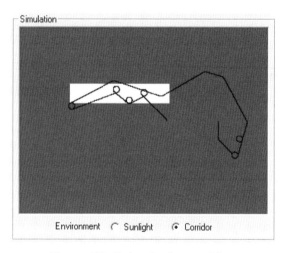

Figure 72. Robot in the corridor.

There is an (invisible) light source but it is not in the corridor. If that were the case this would be a mere repetition of the previous simulation. This does mean that the corridor is in a fixed location for the robots have no way of actively searching for it. The only way for a robot to find the corridor is thus by shear coincidence. And that is exactly what happens here: blind evolution.

This problem is not as simple as it looks for the robots can only make 45 degree turns and to make matters worse they start facing straight down.

This is an example of a program that the genetic algorithm came up with, based on a chromosome length of twenty genes. The previous Figure shows the resulting path.

```
-- JAL 2.1
include 16f877_bert
include robot_bert

B03(45)
B04(45)
B06(10)
B02
B03(45)
B01(10)
B03(45)
B03(45)
B01(10)
B04(45)
B01(10)
B03(45)
B01(10)
B03(45)
B06(10)
B01(10)
B05(10)
B06(10)
B05(10)
B04(45)
```

And surprisingly quick too, in just 50 ruins with a population of just 50.

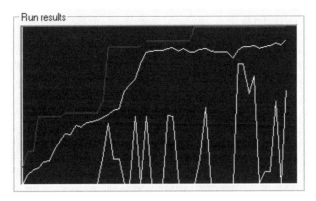

Figure 73. Fitness in a graph.

Because the corridor has no walls the robot doesn't necessarily have to move through it lengthwise, as the next genetic algorithm solution shows. The fitness is lower than in the previous solution (484 against 718), but it is quite original anyway.

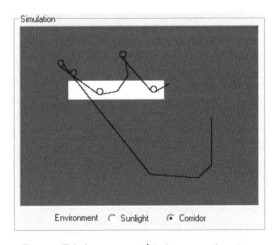

Figure 74. I suppose this is an option too.

Optional 2

With a couple of additions to the JAL program you can display the current behavior block on the LCD display. This is particularly fun to watch in long programs.

8   Expert system

Expert systems, also known as knowledge based systems are an attempt to store the knowledge of human experts on paper or in a computer program. Preferably in such a way that non-experts can use it. This artificial intelligence methodology is mainly intended for situations where human experts might reach a solution but layman would not. The oldest known expert system is approximately 3.500 years old[79]. It consists of a papyrus roll discovered in 1862 by the American Egyptologist Edwin Smith, in a shop in Luxor. The papyrus roll contains questions and instructions regarding the diagnosis and treatment of head injuries[80]. Experts think that this papyrus roll is a copy of an original roll that is believed to be at least 1000 years older.

Figure 75. Fragment of the oldest known expert system[81].

The computer program that Lindsay[82] wrote called DENDRAL[83] is regarded as the first computerized expert system meant for use outside of the academic world. The program's expertise is the translation of mass spectrographic measurements into the structural data of chemical compounds, in other words the identification of unknown substances. As the information contained in the program grew, maintaining it became increasingly difficult by the way.

---

[79] The structure of the text is *if* the patient has these complaints *then* this is the diagnoses and *then* this is the treatment.

[80] Kshettry, V.R., cs., The management of cranial injuries in antiquity and beyond, Neurosurg Focus 23 (1):E8, 2007.

[81] Courtesy of the New York Academy of Medicine Library.

[82] Lindsay, Robert K., B. G. Buchanan, E. A. Feigenbaum, and J. Lederberg (1993), "DENDRAL: A Case Study of the First Expert System for Scientific Hypothesis Formation." Artificial Intelligence 61:209-261.

[83] Lederberg, J., DENDRAL-64: A system for computer construction, enumeration and notation of organic molecules as free structures and cyclic graphs. Interim Report to the National Aeronautics and Space Administration, December 15,1964.

Usually knowledge is stored in expert system as rules, with the format *if... then....* The dialog with an expert systems therefor resembles answering a questionnaire, because the system is filling in a row of *if...then...* questions. This methodology is particularly effective if the subject (the domain) is limited and the questions can be answered unambiguously. For example when analyzing recovered stone tools in archeology[84].

Roger Grace[85] of the University of Essex in England has a nice example of the way an expert systems can be set up. The purpose is the recognition of Norwegian coins (kroner).

The first step is to determine which variables play a role. In this case that would be dimension, color and decoration.

The next step is to assign a range of values to these variables:

dimension	color	decoration
the diameter is >25 mm the diameter is <25 mm	silver bronze	head crown ship lion

Note that properties that apply to all coins are not interesting. All coins are for example round, but that will not help you distinguish between them.

The final step is determining the rules in such a way that each rule only applies to one coin:

if dimension > 25 and the color is bronze and the decoration is ship then the coin is 20K
if dimension < 25 and the color is silver and the decoration is crown then the coin is 1K
if dimension > 25 and the color is silver and the decoration is lion then the coin is 20K

Using these rules you can identify the following coins:

[84] Grace, R. The use of expert systems in lithic analysis. Traces et fonction: les geste retrouvés' Eraul 50, vol. 2; 389-400. Liege 1993
[85] http://web.mac.com/rgrace2/iWeb/ES/example.html

Figure 76. Norwegian Kroner (the left two are silver, the right one is bronze).

You may have noticed that decoration plays a double roll. You could leave the decoration out and in fact simplify the rules to:

> if dimension > 25 and the color is bronze then the coin is 20K
> if dimension < 25 then the coin is 1K
> if dimension > 25 and the color is silver then the coin is 20K

Or you could make use of the decoration only:

> if decoration is ship then the coin is 20K
> if the decoration is crown then the coin is 1K
> if the decoration is lion then the coin is 20K

In that case it might be a good idea to change the decoration "lion" to "lion with crown" because if you only have the 5K coin you could otherwise classify it as "lion" or as "crown".

Redundant questions are useful when the person that is using the program is a layman, so certain questions may be expected to be answered incorrectly due to a lack of knowledge, or because the question was misunderstood.

For computers the rules of an expert system are written as a row of *if... then...*statements, for humans a tree is usually easier to read. You start at the top and follow the questions downward until you reach the end of a branch. This end is then the answer.

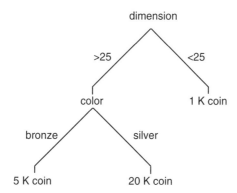

Figure 77. Knowledge tree Norwegian Kroner.

The name expert system is not used very often anymore once the exaggerated expectations of the 1950's and 1960's could not be turned into reality. The methodology as such is very much alive today however. The Windows help system which helps you track down (hardware) issues is an example of such an expert system.

Another area where expert systems are very often used is in robotics. It allows easy and unambiguous robot control using simple rules such as:

>   *if* the left sensor is engaged *then* turn right

As long as the situations that the robot encounters were expected by the programmer, and are thus contained in the expert system, robotic control is indeed very simple. This unambiguous predictability does have its downside however. If the robot meets an unexpected condition it will have no clue what to do. Even something simple as a sensor malfunction may cripple its behavior. Suppose in the previous coin example you are of the opinion that the ship is not a ship but a plant. In that case the expert system can't help you. Unlike for example neural networks which are capable of finding the most likely answer.

Fuzzy variant

A variant of the expert system is the fuzzy expert system. Fuzzy logic takes into account that situations are not always unambiguous. Is the decoration a ship or a plant or is the color copper or bronze? Lay people often call bronze copper or yellow copper.

When the program starts all answers have the same fitness, namely zero. The questions that the fuzzy expert system asks will lead to an increase in one or more fitness values.

At the end of the session the answer with the highest fitness is selected. Depending on the size of the fitness the system can indicate whether the answer is probably right, maybe right et cetera. And it can optionally give a fuzzy logic probability.

Let's assume the maximum fitness is 8, and the best answer had a fitness of 6. This means the fuzzy logic probability is 0.75 (6/8). Note that probability is not the same as chance! A chance of 0.75 means that there is a 75% chance that the answer is <u>completely</u> correct, and a 25% chance that the answer is <u>completely</u> wrong. A probability of 0.75 however means that 75% of the clues you gave lead to this answer. A fine but important distinction.

The fuzzy logic methodology is particularly useful when the information that the program receives is incomplete. That could be because the person answering the questions only has access to incomplete information. For example when the coins in the previous example have been recovered in an excavation and some characteristics are vague or have completely disappeared.

Another option is that the user gives the wrong answers to some questions. He is after all most likely not an expert himself, and may not understand some of the questions. Particularly when laymen need to use the system fuzzy logic is an excellent idea. Just as in the case of mobile robots.

The fuzzy logic rules for the coin example would be:

    if dimension > 25 then add 1 fitness point to coin 20K
                    and add 1 fitness point to coin 5K
    if dimension < 25 then add 1 fitness point to coin 1K

    if the color is bronze then add 1 fitness point to coin 20K
    if the color is silver then add 1 fitness point to coin 5K
                    and add 1 fitness point to coin 1K

    if the decoration is ship then add 1 fitness point to coin 20K
    if the decoration is lion then add 1 fitness point to coin 5K
    if the decoration is crown then add 1 fitness point to coin 1K

Once the questions have been answered, as far as is possible, the program will draw its conclusion based on the fuzzy logic fitness.

    If coin 20K = 3 then the coin is 20 kroner (probability 1)
    If coin 5K = 3 then the coin is 5 kroner (probability 1)
    If coin 1K = 3 then the coin is 1 kroner (probability 1)

If coin 20K = 2 then the coin is 20 kroner (probability 0.7)
If coin 5K = 2 then the coin is 5 kroner (probability 0.7)
If coin 1K = 2 then the coin is 1 kroner (probability 0.7)

Given the importance of the decoration you might consider giving that a higher fitness rating. If you have identified the decoration you have after all a very high probability of knowing which coin it is.

8.1   Tic Tac Toe, or take fifteen

Tic Tac Toe, or noughts[86] and crosses, is a simple game for two players. The goal is to get three crosses or zeros in one line. The playing area has nine fields, which means that perfect players can neither win nor loose, it will always be a draw. For this reason the game is not much fun for adults, but children do fancy playing it. At a young age it is really an exercise in logical thinking.

Tic Tac Toe is regarded as the first graphical computer game, written by Douglas[87] in 1952 on the EDSAC[88] computer of the University of Cambridge.

It is a very suitable game to play using an expert system. The extended version of this game, four on a row, with a board of seven (horizontally) by six (vertically) is by the way also very suitable for an expert systems[89] A perfect first player can always win. We will stick with the simpler game of tic tac toe.

The first step is to consider the strategy, so the rules, that need to be used in order to be a perfect player. The expert system will be the second player, and thus play with the zeros (the first player uses crosses). From now on we will call the players cross and zero.

---

[86] Nought means zero.

[87] Douglas, AS, Noughts and Crosses, University of Cambridge, Phd thesis, 1952.

[88] Electronic Delay Storage Automatic Calculator. You can download a simulator from this site: http://www.dcs.warwick.ac.uk/~edsac/ The artificial intelligence technique the program uses is not clear, but it does play a mean game!

[89] Allis, Victor, A Knowledge-based Approach of Connect Four, Department of Mathematics and Computer Science, Vrije Universiteit, Amsterdam, The Netherlands, Masters Thesis, October 1988

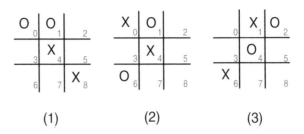

Figure 78. Game situations of tic tac toe.

In game situation one in the previous figure it is clear that zero can win immediately by occupying square 2. In game situation two zero has to play square 8 in order not to lose immediately. This determines the first two rules: win, or prevent the other player from winning. Now it becomes a bit more complicated.

In game situation three it would seem that zero has the following equally interesting moves: three, five and eight. However by playing position five a split is made. That means that zero could now win by playing either three or eight. Of course cross may play first, but cross can only block one of these two moves. So by playing five zero is certain of it's victory. So forcing a split would be rule three.

Rule four is even less obvious. When zero occupies the center position and cross has two positions on the same diagonal a wrong move by zero can lead to a guaranteed loss.

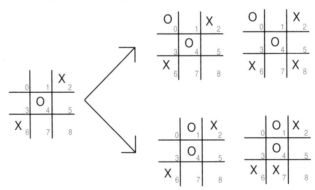

Figure 79. Rule 4 in tic tac toe.

It seems like an innocent game situation but if zero plays on one of the free corners then cross is forced to block the possible victory of zero. In doing so cross causes a split and wins. If for example zero plays square zero, then cross has to play eight. This practically forces cross to win by either playing five or seven (top row in the previous Figure).

So the best option for zero is to play one of the middle fields, for example square one. This forces cross to block on square seven, which means the game ends in a draw (lower row in the previous Figure).

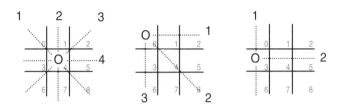

Figure 80. Impact directions of a game board position..

Rule five is simple again: if the center square is empty then play it. This is the only square where a move will count in four directions, maximizing the chance to win.

Rule six is now easy too, select one of the corners, for these count in three directions.

The last rule is basically to select any free square because there are no useful rules left. In fact it means a draw is eminent, but there are still some empty squares left.

The software

Just like in the Norwegian Kroner example the variables need to be defined that the expert system will use to tackle it's decisions. Such a variable could be the content of a row, in such a way that it is easy for the system to tell which rule may be applicable to that particular row. So we will use a value for zero and cross that enables us to evaluate that row quickly

Content	Value
O	10
X	1
. empty	0

Assume that a row contains two zeros. The sum of the fields in this row is twenty. So twenty means: add one zero and you win. If the sum is twelve that means the row contains one zero and two crosses and is thus full.

The playing field is called *Game[x]*, where *x* is the location on the playing field. As you can see in the previous Figures counting starts at zero as is common for computers so the sum of the content of the first row (*SumRow1*) is:

SumRow1 = Game[0] + Game[1] + Game[2]

This way all variables can be defined:

SumRow1 = Game[0] + Game[1] + Game[2]
SumRow2 = Game[3] + Game[4] + Game[5]
SumRow3 = Game[6] + Game[7] + Game[8]
SumColumn1 = Game[0] + Game[3] + Game[6]
SumColumn2 = Game[1] + Game[4] + Game[7]
SumColumn3 = Game[2] + Game[5] + Game[8]
SumDia1 = Game[0] + Game[4] + Game[8]
SumDia2 = Game[2] + Game[4] + Game[6]
SumGame = SumRow1 + SumRow2 + SumRow3

The last variable contains the total of the entire playing field, which will come in handy when rule four is evaluated.

Rule 1: Is an instant win possible?

If SumRow1 == 20 Then SpotInRow (1) end if

If the value of this row is twenty it means that there is just one position free. If zero plays in that position it will have won the game. The question remains which position this actually is, which is solved by the procedure *SpotInRow(x)*.

```
procedure SpotInRow (byte in x) is
    -- find an empty spot in this row
    If x == 1 & Game[0] == 0 Then MyMove = 0 end if
    If x == 1 & Game[1] == 0 Then MyMove = 1 end if
    If x == 1 & Game[2] == 0 Then MyMove = 2 end if
    If x == 2 & Game[3] == 0 Then MyMove = 3 end if
    If x == 2 & Game[4] == 0 Then MyMove = 4 end if
    If x == 2 & Game[5] == 0 Then MyMove = 5 end if
    If x == 3 & Game[6] == 0 Then MyMove = 6 end if
    If x == 3 & Game[7] == 0 Then MyMove = 7 end if
    If x == 3 & Game[8] == 0 Then MyMove = 8 end if
End procedure
```

The first *if/then* statement of this procedure basically says "*if* the free position is in row one, *and* the first position in this row is empty, *then* the move must be made in the first position". The same question is repeated for every line and every position. Technically it would have looked much more professional if I had used a few simple loops rather than a row of almost identical statements. The reason for not doing that is that this row of *if/then* statements is more in line with the expert system methodology, and it makes it easier to expand with new rules.

Of course rule one should not be tested for *SumRow1* only, but for all rows, columns and diagonals. So there is also a procedure for finding an empty spot in a column and a diagonal, as you can see in the source.

Rule 2: Prevent an instant defeat?

If SumRow1 == 2 Then SpotInRow (1) end if

Rule two should only be executed if rule one proved unsuccessful. At the beginning of the analyses a variable is defined (and given the value 100) which will contain the move the program will make, called *MyMove*. If this variable is still 100 a move is yet to be found (after all the highest possible move is 8).

If *SumRow1* is two it means that this row contains two crosses and needs to be blocked immediately to prevent an instant defeat. Again you can use the procedure *SpotInRow(x)* to find the proper location for this move. The question is repeated for all rows, columns and diagonals.

Rule 3: Is it possible to split?

If (SumRow1 + SumColumn2 == 20) & Game[1] == 0 Then MyMove = 1 end if

At first we check to see if the sum of the first row and column is twenty. That would mean that each row and column has one zero. Two zeros in one row or column is impossible because that would have resulted in a move according to rule one (and an instant win).

Next we need to check if position zero (the cross point of the first row and the first column) is empty. If it is, than this is the move the program will make.

If it was not empty it means that our zero is on that location, because then it would be counted in the row as well as the column, which would also result in a sum of twenty.

This question is repeated for each square on the playing board

Rule 4: Is there a middle position available with free corners?

If SumGame==12 & SumDia1==12 & Game[4]==10 Then MyMove = 3 end if

This question consists of three parts. The first part checks to see if the entire board only contains one zero and two crosses. The second parts checks to see if these are all on one diagonal. And the third part checks to see if the center one is a zero. If this is all true then position three must be available, and would be a good move to make. This question is repeated for the other diagonal.

Rule 5: Take the center position if it is available.

If Game[4] == 0 Then MyMove = 4 end if

This requires no further explanation.

Rule 6: Take a corner position if one is available.

If Game[0] == 0 Then MyMove = 0 end if

This question is repeated for each of the corner positions.

Rule 7: Take a random free position.

```
t = 0
For 9 loop
    If Game[t] == 0 Then MyMove = t end if
    t = t + 1
end loop
```

This rule could have been phrased as seven questions. At this point that would be rather useless. There is simply no intelligent move to be made but the game isn't finished yet so we are basically filling empty spaces. No matter what the other expert rules are, this final one never changes, though it may get a higher number if other rules are placed in between the previous ones.

At this point *MyMove* should have a value other than 100. If that is not the case the microcontroller wasn't able to make a move because the playing field is full.

The hardware

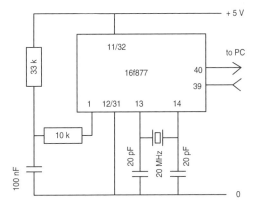

Figure 81. Tic tac toe hardware.

The schematic and the picture of the breadboard can be used to build this project. The connection with the PC using the Wisp programmer is a requirement in this project.

Figure 82. Tic tac toe hardware.

Instructions

Build the hardware and download the JAL program into the microcontroller. Do not disconnect the Wisp programmer. Start the Visual Basic program on your PC. Click on the "new game" button. You start and play with the crosses. Select a position on the playing field and click the mouse button to make your move.

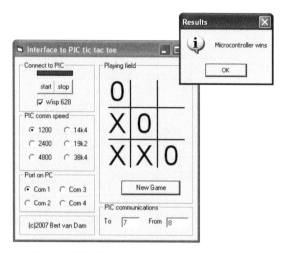

Figure 83. The expert system in action.

In the square at the bottom you can see which number is sent to the microcontroller. The adjacent square shows the reply. These numbers are purely informational, the answer from the microcontroller is also shown as a zero on the playing field

You know the strategy the program is using so if anyone can win from the microcontroller that should be you....

You will need this same JAL program and the same hardware for the Menace project (section 11.3) where it will play against an autonomous learning program designed in 1960.

Optional 1

Even though the program tries to force a split on the opponent (rule 3) it doesn't attempt to protect itself against splits. Is it possible for a human player to exploit this?

Optional 2

A game where a player never wins becomes boring rather quickly. Because it is an expert program it is very easy to add rules. Perhaps it is an interesting idea to add some "human error" to the program by allowing it to make a mistake every once in a while. Now the human player has to pay close attention because this just might be the game where the microcontroller makes a mistake.

Optional 3

The expert program plays a defensive game because the human player starts. Offensive play can lead inexperienced opponents to game positions they can't win[90]. A few rules need to be added for this. Of course this makes no difference when playing against experienced players.

Optional 4

The game "four on a row" can also be played using an expert system. In this game the first player by the way always wins (assuming errorless play). Allis's[91] rules, in combination with the basic program structure in this section, allow you to write a "four on a row" program for your microcontroller.

Optional 5 Take 15

If Tic Tac Toe begins to bore you the same software can be used to play a different game: Take 15. The game is designed as a bit of a joke by game designer Fuchs[92], and works as follows. Nine playing cards are laid out on the table in a row, with numbers one to nine. The two players take turns in taking one card. The winner is the player who can make 15 with the cards in his hand. If for example you have the cards 2, 3, 4 and 9 in your hand then you win because you can make 15: $2 + 4 + 9 = 15$.

Figure 84. Take 15[93].

[90] Aycock, R, How to Win at Tic-Tac-Toe, 2002, Pdf limited publication.
[91] Allis, Victor, A Knowledge-based Approach of Connect Four, Department of Mathematics and Computer Science, Vrije Universiteit, Amsterdam, The Netherlands, Masters Thesis, October 1988
[92] Fuchs, Jesse. www.eludication.org Very worth your while to take a look at this site.
[93] Carddesign David Ballot, released under the Lesser GNU Public License.

It is a nice but rather simple game. Perhaps you have noticed after a while that the game tends to always end in a draw. The reason for this is simple: this game in an isomorph of Tic Tac Toe. A game which looks and feels different but uses the exact same game engine. The nine playing cards represent a Tic Tac Toe playing board and form a magical square. This means the sum of all rows, columns and diagonals has the exact same value, in this case fifteen.

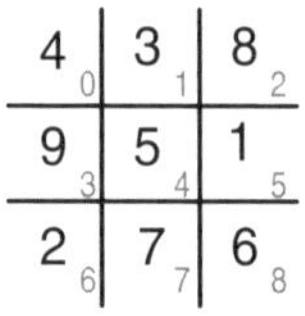

Figure 85. Take 15 on a Tic Tac Toe playing board.

This means that trying to get 15 with three cards is equivalent with getting three crosses or zeros in a column, row or diagonal. The card example given before $(2 + 4 + 9 = 15)$ is simply the first column.

If you own Visual Basic you can adapt the graphical user interface of the program and turn it into a Take 15 game. Because no-one will recognize this to be Tic Tac Toe the microcontroller should be able to win for quite a while.

8.2   The programmer

The question for the expert system is quite simple. A microcontroller is flashing an LED. A second microcontroller also has an LED and has to flash it in the exact same frequency by following the LED of the first microcontroller. It can do this by measuring the light intensity of the LED using and LDR, and comparing it with a threshold value. So for this microcontroller the following rules apply:

> if LDR value < threshold then my LED must be off
> if LDR value > threshold then my LED must be on

So the question is: write a JAL program with these rules, and the correct value for the variable *threshold*. A human programmer might solve this problem as follows:

1. Make the LED of the first microcontroller flash.
2. Place the LDR near the LED.
3. Write a JAL program that contains the previous rules with a random value for threshold and see what happens.

4. Adapt the threshold and repeat step three until the LED is flashing in synch with the LED of the first microcontroller.
5. The last JAL program you made is the answer to the question.

Step four contains the actual expert knowledge. If your own LED is always off then the threshold is too low, because the LDR value never drops below it. If the LED is always on then the threshold is too high because the LDR value never raises above it. So the expert rules are:

> if "my own LED is always off" then "the threshold needs to be raised"
> if "my own LED is always on" then "the threshold needs to be lowered"
> if "my own LED is flashing" then "the threshold is exactly right"

For an expert systems these rules are very simple and could easily be incorporated into a JAL program. The special thing about this project is that a Visual Basic program on the PC will act as an expert, and will actually program the microcontroller by itself without human intervention.

The program will go through the exact same five steps that a human expert would go through. This project only works if you use the Wisp programmer because it requires both in-circuit programming and pass-through functionality.

1. The Visual Basic program starts by writing a JAL program and storing it on the hard drive. The next step is to compile it into HEX code, and use the Wisp programmer to download it into the microcontroller. The JAL program will start automatically, check the LDR value for five seconds and compare it to the threshold value. If the threshold is set correctly the LDR value should be at least once above the threshold, and at least once below it during that five second period.

    > -- *mark whether the resistance has been both*
    > -- *below and above the threshold*
    > if resist < threshold then LEDoff = 1 end if
    > if resist > threshold then LEDon = 1 end if

2. The results of this test are send back to the PC. In the meantime the JAL program will attempt to flash its LED in synch with the other LED, which at this point will most likely fail.

3. The Visual Basic program evaluates the data it has received from the microcontroller.

LEDon = 1	LEDoff = 1	suggested action
yes	no	increase threshold (+15)
no	yes	reduce threshold (-15)
yes	yes	done!

If the suggested action is "done" then the Visual Basic program will stop, because apparently the JAL program is functioning as it should and the LED is now flashing. When the JAL program is not running correctly the threshold needs to be adjusted, particularly the line *threshold = 150*.

4. Then the Visual Basic program loops back to step one and repeats these steps, until the JAL program works perfectly.

Software

The Visual Basic program uses batch files to start other programs such as the compiler (jalv2.exe) and the downloader (xwisp2.exe). Windows is a multitasking program. This means that when the batch files are started the Visual Basic program will not pause but continue to run and thus may "overtake" the batch files. Unfortunately there is no simple way to check if a batch file has stopped running. However compiling a source doesn't take very long so if the Visual Basic program waits for three seconds the compiler should be done:

```
'call compile batch file
commando$ = Directory$ + "\jalcompile.bat " + FileName$ + ".jal"
retval = Shell(commando$, 1)

'wait three seconds for compilation to complete
Duration! = Timer + 3
Do Until Timer > Duration!
  dummy = DoEvents()
Loop
```

If your computer is slower you need to increase the three second wait. Downloading to the microcontroller may take a lot longer, but that process uses the COM port. Since only one program can use a COM port at any given time, all we need to do is attempt to open the port. If that succeeds the download has apparently finished. If it doesn't succeed just wait two seconds and try again. "Doesn't succeed" means that Windows will generate an error which would abort the Visual Basic program. An error trapping routine is used to prevent this from happening:

```
'send to xwisp2 downloader
commando$ = Directory$ + "\jalprogram.bat " + FileName$ + ".hex"
retval = Shell(commando$, 1)

'wait for the com port to be released before continuing
'wait 2 second for the programmer to start
Duration! = Timer + 2
Do Until Timer > Duration!
  dummy = DoEvents()
Loop

'enable error trapping
On Error GoTo Waiting

'(attempt to)enable communications
MSComm1.PortOpen = True

'turn progress indicator green
Shape3.FillColor = &H8000&

'close communications
MSComm1.PortOpen = False

'disable error trappping
On Error GoTo 0
```

At the end of this routine the error trapping routine is disabled again to allow other errors to be noticed. The error routine itself is at the end of the module:

```
'exit sub to prevent entering the error routine
Exit Sub

Waiting:
 'wait one second
 Duration! = Timer + 1
 Do Until Timer > Duration!
   dummy = DoEvents()
 Loop

 'And try again at the same statement that caused the error
 Resume
```

The batch files that this Visual Basic program uses are part of the download package. If you unzipped the package to the recommended location you can use the batch files as they are. If you used a different location or a different programmer you will need to modify path and programmer data in each of the batch files.

Hardware

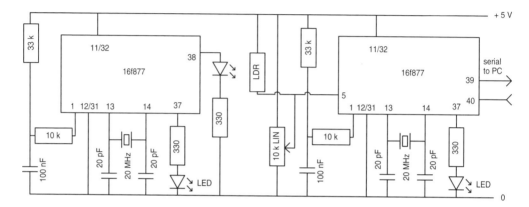

Figure 86. The programmer schematic.

The hardware can be built using the schematic and the picture. The use of an in-circuit programmer with pass-through functionality such as the Wisp programmer is a requirement. The Wisp could in fact be considered part of the hardware.

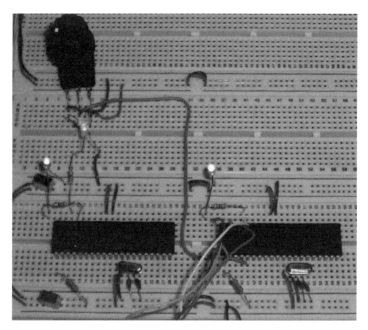

Figure 87. The programmer in the breadboard.

Instructions

The Wisp programmer is an essential part of this project. After you have loaded the flashing LED program into the microcontroller on the left you must connect the Wisp to the microcontroller on the right, and leave it there. You do <u>not</u> need to download any software into this microcontroller (the Visual Basic program will do that for you)

The batch files that you use must be in the directory shown in the Visual Basic program. If you use the default directory c:\picai\tmp\ you do not need to change anything: the batch files are already in this directory.

Connect the power to the project and start the Visual Basic program on the PC. You will now see the following window on the PC screen.

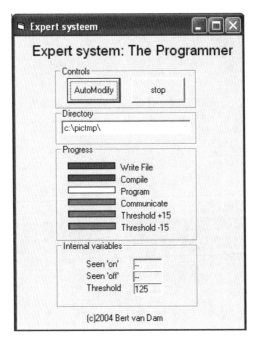

Figure 88. The programmer in action.

Now click on "AutoModify". The red bars on the screen one by one turn yellow, then green and then they all turn red again.

color	meaning
red	still to do
yellow	in progress
green	completed

After a while the LED on the microcontroller on the right side will start to flash in synch with the other LED. That means that the Visual Basic program has done its job correctly.

Optional

When the JAL program is ready it still contains a section of code which checks the threshold value and wants to communicate with the PC. At the moment this code is dormant, but it would be nicer if the final version that the PC downloads doesn't contain this section of code anymore. This should be relatively easy to do since the Visual Basic program knows when it is done, so all that is needed is to add one extra final step.

146

9 Cellular automata

In 1940 Ulam[94] tried to model the growth of crystals using squared paper and a pencil. Depending on the circumstances the crystal model would grow a square in a certain direction. By choosing the right formulas the growth pattern would look very realistic. Without a computer however this is of course a very cumbersome operation.

During that same time period von Neumann is dreaming of self replicating robots. Robots that turn raw materials into parts, and then use these parts to assemble copies of themselves, utterly impossible at the time. But when he sees the work of Ulam he realizes that with a few simple modifications to the formulas the crystals will change shape. The models on the squared paper change, split and even move. This is exactly what he is looking for, not with real parts but as an abstract model. He calls this model cellular automata[95].

Von Neumann is experimenting with squared paper and physical objects like tokens on a Go board in an attempt to find a convenient way to use cellular automata. But no matter what he tries it remains cumbersome and error prone. The onset of the computer has a dramatic effect, and in 1960 Conway[96] uses cellular automata concepts in "The Game of Life".

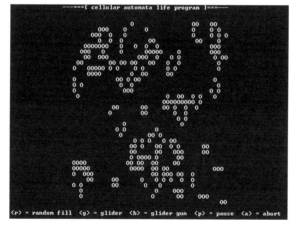

Figure 89. Game of Life program modeled after Conway[97].

---

[94] Stanisław Marcin Ulam (April 13, 1909 – May 13, 1984)
[95] Neumann, John von, Theory of Self-Reproducing Automata, posthumous publication by Arthur W. Burks, University of Illinois Press Champaign, IL, USA, 1966
[96] Scientific American, October 1970, Martin Gardner's "Mathematical Games" column on John Horton Conway's Game Of Life.
[97] Van Dam, Bert, November 2000.

It is not a game that you can actually play, it is a game where you watch an artificial world evolve. It works as follows. A cell (a square on the squared paper) can either be alive of dead. Alive means the cell has value of one, dead means the cell has value of zero. To determine which cells live and which cells die a set of rules is used:

1. A dead cell surrounded by three live cells will come alive (there is a total of eight cells surround any given cell).
2. A living cell stays alive when exactly two or three other living cells surround it.
3. A living cell will die if it is surrounded by less than two or more than three living cells.

The next Figure shows a few steps of this automation. A cross represents a living cell, so an empty cell is dead.

Cell number 14 has value 1, so it is alive (represented by the cross). The surrounding cells are 7, 8, 9, 13, 15, 19, 20 and 21. Of all these cells only one of them, cell 20, is alive. That means rule three applies and thus cell 14 dies. The same calculation for cell 20 results in two living cells. This means rule two applies and cell 20 stays alive. Cell 19 is dead, but three living cells surround it. So rule one applies and this cell comes alive. Using this technique for all cells in the grid on the left this will result in the grid on the right.[98]

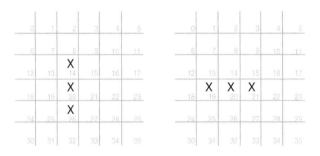

Figure 90. Game of Life.

As long as the game is running you cannot do anything, but you can select an interesting starting pattern. It is for example possible to design a starting pattern which repeats the same movement over and over again. Let us see what would happen to the example in the previous figure if we let the automation run one step longer.

---

[98] New crosses are placed after <u>all</u> cells in the grid have been evaluated. This way the processing sequence of the cells has no impact on the result.

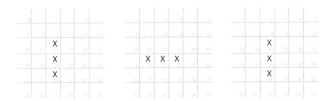

Figure 91. A blinker.

As you can see the grid has returned to the original pattern. This is called a blinker. Also quite interesting is a pattern that moves across the screen, a so called glider.

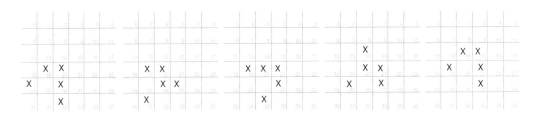

Figure 92. A glider.

Another way to play with this is by changing the rules. For example the number of neighboring cells that is required for a particular cell to become alive, or the way the neighboring cells are counted. You could even use weighted counting, where some neighboring cells are more important than others are. You also don't need to limit yourself to cells that can only be dead or alive. By allowing other numbers than zero and one and representing these numbers as colors beautiful pictures can be made.

Mirek[99] wrote a very nice program to try out these ideas. It contains dozens of examples to watch and modify according to your own needs.

Until now we have assumed a two dimensional grid. This is used very often because it can conveniently be represented on a computer screen, which is two dimensional too. Of course the grid can also be one-dimensional, for example for the simulation of traffic congestion[100]. Or three dimensional, for the simulation of liquids, or in fact multidimensional for abstract applications.

---

[99] Mirek's Cellebration, MCell 4.20, www.mirekw.com/ca/index.html
[100] Hämäläinen, Arto, Studies of Traffic Situations using Cellular Automata, Department of Engineering Physics and Mathematics, Helsinki University of Technology, PhD thesis, Oct 2006.

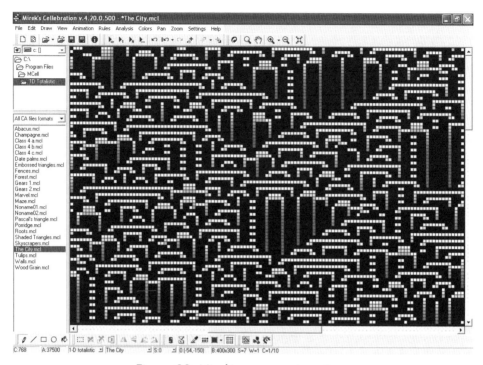

Figure 93. Mirek's program in action.

In cellular automata three settings are required:

1. The number of dimensions of the grid
2. The rules to be used
3. The starting pattern

Von Neumann's idea that robots could build other robots has by the way partially been turned into reality. In many factories robots are used to carry out heavy or tedious operations, and that includes factories that manufacture robots. The dream that this would function all by itself has perhaps come yet another step closer with the advent of nano technology!

Cellular automata are mainly used in pattern recognition, encryption and simulation of for example liquid flow[101] and the growth patterns of cities[102][103], and they are quite successful

[101] Vichiniac G.Y. (1984), Simulating Physics with Cellular Automata, Physica 10D, 96-116

[102] Clarke, K.C, cs., 1996, A Self-Modifying Cellular Automaton Model of Historical Urbanization in the San Francisco Bay Area, Environment and Planning B, Santa Fe, NM

150

in it too. There is a certain overlap with emergent behavior. The wave for example could easily be simulated with a cellular automation, with rules such as these:

1. A cell will become alive if a single cell next to it is alive.
2. A cell will die if two cells on one side are alive.

The unexpected collapse of a bridge in Minneapolis (USA) in 2007 even resulted in an inquiry to use cellular automata to come up with alternate bridge designs. These are expected to be less prone to sudden collapse because they would have a more irregular super structure.[104]

9.1   The artist

Yet another application of cellular automata is art. Figure 93 which has a screenshot of Mirek's program looks very nice in color, and in fact it even moves. In this project a microcontroller will make a very simple moving picture using a cellular automation (often abbreviated to CA).

The basis of the CA program is an array where each element in the array is a cell. Each cell is linked to a location on the screen. A second array is used to determine the new situation. Once that is completed the arrays are switched and the new array is shown. The easiest way would be to use two dimensional arrays but JAL doesn't support this. So we will start with a one dimensional array and fold it up. And of course we need two of these.

The larger the arrays the bigger the picture on the screen. The main problem is the limited amount of memory in the 16F877(A). To make matters worse this memory is divided over four banks[105]. So the two array which we will call 0 and 1 will each be split in two parts called A and B, to make everything fit. So we end up with four arrays:

```
var byte CAt0A[80]
var byte CAt0B[75]

var byte CAt1A[80]
var byte CAt1B[75]
```

[103] Engelen, Guy, cs. Integrating Constrained Cellular Automata Models, GIS and Decision Support Tools for Urban Planning and Policy Making, Decision Support Systems in Urban Planning, chapter 8. Spon Press; 1 edition (April 21, 1998), 0419210504
[104] Rogers, A, The future of bridges: self-replicating and weird-looking, Wired-Science, August 6, 2007.
[105] Bert van Dam, PIC Microcontrollers, 50 projects for beginners and experts, Elektor, ISBN 978-0-905705-70-5 page 228.

Arrays t1 are the new versions of arrays t0 (t represents time). With these arrays a grid of 16 by 9 cells can be made. Not very large, but large enough for some interesting applications. Each cell is in the center of a group of nine cells. Because our array is folded into a rectangle it isn't obvious which cells are neighbors of each other.

Let us start with cell zero in the first array. This cell can be regarded as the upper left corner of a block of nine cells. If that cell is called n then the 8 neighbors are n+1, n+2, n+16, n+17, n+18, n+32, n+33 and n+34. If one of these numbers is larger than 79 we need to move over to the second half of the array, simply by deducting 80 from each number[106].

58	59	60	61	62	63	**64**	**65**	**66**	67	68	69	70	71	72	73
74	75	76	77	78	79	**0**	**1**	**2**	3	4	5	6	7	8	9
10	11	12	13	14	15	**16**	**17**	**18**	19	20	21	22	23	24	25
26	27	28	29	30	31	32	33	34	35	36	37	38	39	40	41

If we do this for example for the section of grid shown above, right on the border of the two array parts, then this would be the result:

n = 64	array 1	array 2	cell name
64	64		NW
64+1=65	65		NN
64+2=66	66		NE
64+16=80		80-80=0	WW
64+17=81		81-80=1	ME
64+18=82		82-80=2	EE
64+32=96		96-80=16	SW
64+33=97		97-80=17	SS
64+34=98		98-80=18	SE

You may have noted the new column on the right-hand side. This column contains the abbreviations of the directions of the wind rose, which is the internationally recognized way of naming each cell in our block of nine. The ME in the center is not an abbreviation, it simple means "me".

---

[106] Attention: the array is 80 long, but counting starts at 0. So the last array index is 79.

In JAL adding the content of the block of nine can be programmed like this:

```
procedure CalcSum(byte in g, byte in w) is
    --find the right array, retrieve the value, multiply by weight and add to sum
    If g > 79 Then
        Sum = Sum + (CAtOB[g - 80] * w)
    Else
        Sum = Sum + (CAtOA[g] * w)
    End If
End procedure
```

A new variable has been introduced, the w. This is a weighing factor, that can be used to give the cells a different weight. Apart from using it as an actual weight you can also use it to eliminate certain cells from the calculation, simply by multiplying the unwanted cells by weight zero.

In this project we will use an automata designed by Fredkin[107] with this rule:

NW0,NN1,NE0,WW1,ME1,EE1,SW0,SS1,SE0,RS1,RS3,RS5,RB1,RB3,RB5

NW is the position of the cell (see the previous table) and the number behind it represents the weighing factor. In the case of NW the factor is zero, so the content of NW is not used. The abbreviations RS and RB are Rule to Stay alive and Rule for Birth (become alive). If the participating cells (so with weight 1) are added up the central cell (ME) will stay alive if the sum is 1, 3 or 5. A dead cell will come alive (be born) if the sum is 1, 3 or 5 too.

Two of the three settings for this CA have now been determined: the grid dimensions and the rules. The only setting remaining is the starting pattern. We will start with a single living cell: number 71.

---

[107] Dewdney, A.K., The Armchair Universe, W. H. Freeman and Company, New York, 1988. (ISBN 0-716-71938-x), page 24 ev.

The hardware

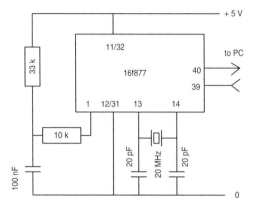

Figure 94. The artist's hardware.

The hardware can be built using the schematic and the picture. The use of an in-circuit programmer with pass-through functionality such as the Wisp programmer is a requirement, it could in fact be considered to be part of the hardware.

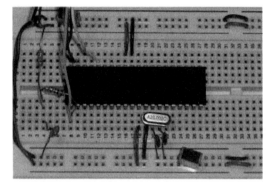

Figure 95. The artist's hardware.

Instructions

Build the hardware and download the JAL program into the microcontroller, leave the Wisp connected and powered. Start the Visual Basic program on the PC. Click on "Start" to connect to the microcontroller. Click on "New" to start a new cycle. In the middle of the window a purple square appears. This is the first, and currently only, living cell.

Now click "Get Next" to order the JAL program to calculate the next cycle of the automation. At the right of the button the text "Please wait" appears until the data has been calculated and send back to the PC. Each time you press the "Get Next" button a new cycle is calculated and displayed.

After four cycli a special event occurs. The screen is almost empty again, except for three squares. This is an example of Von Neumann's self replication. Starting with a single square this CA turns it into three. Effectively it has made two copies of itself.

After seven cycli the picture in the next Figure is created. Then the screen is full and our little artist makes a mess out of it. Never the less an impressive sequence.

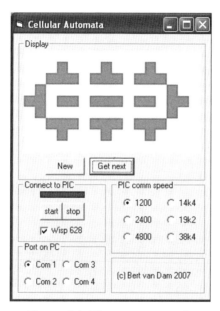

Figure 96. The artist at work.

Optional 1

The JAL program is very flexible. You can try many different CA's simply by changing only three sections. The starting pattern:

```
-- set starting condition ("seed")
CAt0A[71] = 1
```

The weights:

```
-- set weights this is part one of the cellular automata formula
W1 = 0
W2 = 1
W3 = 0
W4 = 1
W5 = 1
W6 = 1
W7 = 0
W8 = 1
W9 = 0
```

And the actual rules for living and dying:

```
-- this is part two of the cellular automata formula
If Sum == 1 | Sum == 3 | Sum == 5 Then
    serial_sw_write(1)
    If g > 79 Then
        CAt1B[g - 80] = 1
    Else
        CAt1A[g] = 1
    End If
Else
    serial_sw_write(0)
    If g > 79 Then
        CAt1B[g - 80] = 0
    Else
        CAt1A[g] = 0
    End If
End If
```

Optional 2

In this project we choose to show the picture on the screen of the PC. It is also possible to show the picture in LEDs. The LEDs can be mounted in a two dimensional area, or even a three dimensional space.

For practical reasons you can reduce the size to 5 x 5 LEDs (since you have 33 outputs available) or you can use shift registers to expand the number of outputs. It is certainly worth while to take a look at the work done by artist Clar[108].

Optional 3

The cellular automation in this project uses the Fredkin[109] principle. This means that any starting pattern you choose will repeat itself twice, or rather: be copied twice. The larger the pattern the longer this takes. You can start with a slightly larger pattern and see what happens. The next Figure shows a simulation of Fredkins rule in Mirek's program.

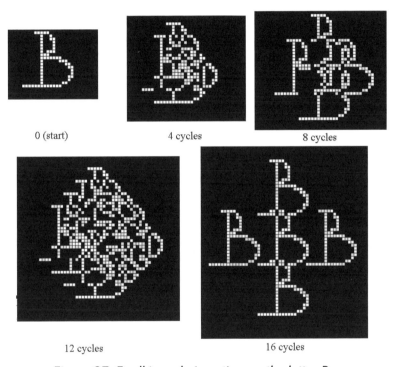

0 (start)   4 cycles   8 cycles

12 cycles   16 cycles

Figure 97. Fredkins rule in action on the letter B.

---

[108] Clar, James, American artist, website www.jamesclar.com
[109] Fredkins "two-state parity rule" means that a cell becomes one when an odd number of cells in the group of nine is one, and zero when an even number of cells in this group is one. This rule makes copy after copy of the original starting pattern. The larger the starting pattern the more cycles are required for the reproduction.

Optional 4

You can use much larger arrays and thus much larger pictures when you use flash memory. This is the memory where the actual microcontroller program is in. How to do that is outside the scoop of this book, but if you own a copy of "PIC Microcontrollers, 50 projects for beginners and experts" you can try to make a picture of 50 x 50 cells[110].

9.2   The musician

As early as 1951 the Olson-Belar Composing Machine was capable of completely automatically generating music based on random numbers. It was not supposed to spontaneously compose something beautiful, but to help composers in their search for new and interesting sounds[111]. It didn't take long before a computer program made by Hiller[112] in 1957 wrote the first automatically composed piece of music: the string Quartet #4. Affectionately called the Illiac Suite, after the computer that ran the program.

In this project we will make a microcontroller play music based on a one-dimensional cellular automation loosely based on the work of Reiners[113] and Burraston[114]. In a one-dimensional CA all cells are in a single row. The position of any cell is therefor solely dependent on the cells next to it. Note that this doesn't have to be limited to just one neighbor: you might envision a CA which depends on for example five neighbors on the left and four on the right. Because the progress of the automata is difficult to follow several cycli are often displayed as rows on a screen. This is only meant for ease of analyses, previous rows have no impact on the current row, and cannot be changed.

For one-dimensional automata where each cell is only dependent on one single neighbor on the left and one on the right a single number is used to record the rule. This number shows what has to be done in every single situation. There are eight possible situations that are always listed in the same order. The result of each position can either be a zero or a one. By putting these zeros and one's in a row and treating them as binary numbers the rule number can be determined. For rule 150 (10010110) this looks like this:

---

[110] van Dam, PIC Microcontrollers, 50 projects for beginners and experts, Elektor ISBN 978-0-905705-70-5 page 222.

[111] Olson, H.F., cs, Aid to Music Composition Employing a Random-Probability System, The Journal of the Acoustical Society of America -- June 1961 -- Volume 33, Issue 6, p. 862

[112] Hiller, L. and Isaacson, L. (1959) Experimental Music. New York :McGraw Hill.

[113] Reiners, P, Cellular Automata and Music, Using the Java language for algorithmic music composition, IB DeveloperWorks, May 2004, http://www.ibm.com/developerworks/

[114] Burraston, D, cs., Cellular Automata in MIDI based Computer Music, Proceedings of the International Computer Music Conference, 2004

| 1 | 0 | 0 | 1 | 0 | 1 | 1 | 0 = 150 |

Figure 98. Rule 150.

Using this rule number the calculation of the result of any given pattern is very simple. First add the content of the three cells using this formula:

index = 4 x (cell left) + 2 x (this cell) + 1 x (cell right)

The content of the new cell is the rightmost bit of *nstate*, where *nstate* is obtained by shifting the rule right by the number of positions indicated by *index:*

nstate = rule >> index

As an example the calculation for the second state from the right where the two left cells are white (0) and the right cell is black (1).

index = 4 x 0 + 2 x 0 + 1 x 1 = 1

Based on rule 150 *nstate* will be:

nstate = 150 >> 1 = 75

In binary this is easier to understand:

nstate = 10010110 >> 1 = 1001011

So the rightmost bit of *nstate* is 1 (so black), which is indeed correct. In JAL this is handled as follows:

```
counter = counter + 1
index = 4 * CAt0[counter-1] + 2 * CAt0[counter] + CAt0[counter + 1]
nstate = rule >> index
CAt1[counter]=nbit
```

where the variables are defined for a cellular automation which is 91 cells wide:

```
var byte CAt0[91]
var byte CAt1[91]
var byte rule, nstate, index, counter
var bit nbit at nstate:0     -- rightmost bit
```

It is not so difficult anymore to run this automation, similar to the previous project. Rule 150 looks like this when graphically displayed. Remember that this is a one-dimensional automation, so what you see is in fact the history of all single lines displayed under each other.

Figure 99. The history of rule 150.

As you see the starting point is not in the middle and the automation crashes into the sides quite quickly. The effect is that the CA shows a bit of irregular behavior that makes the music much more exiting. There is a certain amount of pattern repetition, which causes familiarity in music and makes it sound "nice". But at the same time there is a lot of change, which makes the music more exciting, more surprising.

Before these numbers can be tuned into music however the CA must be connected to musical notes, or rather: tones. We have chosen to generate one single tone for each line, because polyphone music would be a bit too much for the microcontroller. Each line is 91 cells wide, and every cell contains a 0 or a 1, so in fact we have 91 bits to choose from[115]. If eight bits are selected then together these form a byte, which can be used as a reference to a certain tone.

Rainers uses the following selection method for the eight bits. Based on a certain starting point he alternatingly takes a bit from the left and the right at an increasing distance from the starting point, as shown in the next figure.

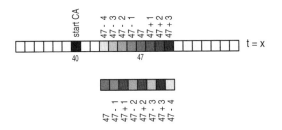

Figure 100. Generating a byte from bits around cell 47.

Another selection would of course result in another number, and thus another tone. I like the sound best when the selection does not coincide with the CA starting cell. If the starting cell is 40 I particularly like selections centered around cells 43, 45 or 47.

The sound byte variable is called *sound*, and is converted into actual sound by connecting a loudspeaker to a pin and switching this pin on and off in the right frequency. This has to be done very accurately because you can hear even the tiniest of deviations. For that reason an interrupt is used, in particular the timer0 interrupt. How often this interrupt occurs, and thus what the frequency of the tone is, is determined by the starting point of timer0[116]. The closer the starting point is to 255 the sooner the interrupt will occur.

---

[115] JAL doesn't have bit arrays, so we are using bytes.
[116] How this is done exactly is outside the scope of this book. More explanation on the timer0 interrupt, making music and many other projects can be found in the book PIC Microcontrollers, 50 projects for beginners and experts, Elektor ISBN 978-0-905705-70-5

```
procedure make_a_sound is
    pragma interrupt

    if T0if then
        -- switch pin to make sound
        flag = ! flag
        pin_c2 = flag
        -- use correct frequency
        tmr0 = sound
        -- clear TOIF to re-enable timer interrupts
        T0if = 0
    end if
end procedure
```

It is by the way a good idea to make the staring point for the timer0 interrupt not too high otherwise the microcontroller will not have enough time for the rest of the program resulting in a crash.

A length of 250 mS for each sound makes the music sound quite nice.

The hardware

The hardware can be built using the schematic and the picture. The loudspeaker is scavenged from an old headset. It uses about 1.54 mA, so it can be directly connected to the microcontroller. If your loudspeaker consumes more power care should be taken. The coil in the speaker can generate a reverse current that can damage the microcontroller. In that case a resistor of for example 100 ohm is advised. Currents over 2 mA are to be avoided, if your speaker consumes more you must use a driver. A 1k variable resistor takes care of the volume control.

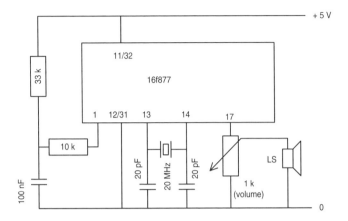

Figure 101. Schematic CA musician.

Figure 102. The project in operation.

Instructions

Build the hardware and download the program into the microcontroller. The music will start immediately. Rule 150 can generate several different pieces of music by changing the starting point of the cellular automation by shifting it left or right. The collisions of the CA against the boundaries (the walls so to speak) cause many different patterns.

You can also change the center point of the music byte. It is now close to the starting point, but you could set it at any different point to your liking. It takes some experimenting to get music that you like.

And of course you can change the CA rule, for example to rule 30, which is also very nice. Be warned that many rules eventually end in a fixed pattern and thus in a single tone.

Optional 1

All notes have the exact same length, in fact 250 mS. You could use the same technique that generates the tone to generate the length of that tone. You will need just three bits to get a decent variation. This will spice up your music.

Optional 2

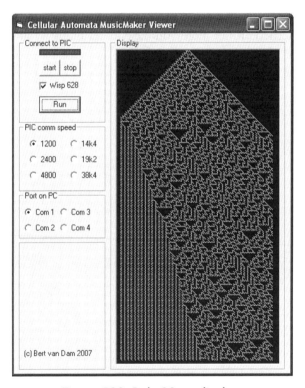

Figure 103. Rule 30 on display.

It is not possible to communicate with the PC and generate music at the same time. This is because the timer0 interrupt is constantly interrupting the communications through the Wisp programmer. In the download package you will find a special program that does the exact same thing as our musician, but in stead of making music it displays the patterns on the PC. Download this program into the microcontroller, leave the Wisp connected and powered and start the PC program. Click on "Start" to start the communication and then on "Run". If you discovered a nice pattern you can transfer the rule and starting position into the music program to see (or rather listen to) what it sounds like.

Optional 3

It is also possible to let the microcontroller determine by itself what rule and starting position should be used. Use random numbers and let the microcontroller surprise you.

Optional 4

The Belgium artist and performer Raes has connected a microcontroller to sirens and gave performances with it, though without CA. With the information on his website[117] you can give your microcontroller more volume and definitely a rather special sound!

---

[117] Gofdried-Willem Raes, http://logosfoundation.org/instrum-god.html, the Sire robot can be found here: logosfoundation.org/instrum_gwr/sire.html A performance of this robot is on YouTube youtube.com/watch?v=w88kg2fHb0M

10   Subsumption architecture

In 1985 Brooks[118] wrote an internal memo at the Massachusetts Institute of Technology (MIT) called "A robust layered control mechanism for mobile robots". It will change the direction of robotics research in the field of artificial intelligence for years to come. In 1999 the Japanese manufacturer Sony releases a robotic dog,[119,120] the AIBO[121], based on this technique. It is the first intelligent robot for the general public and it has been sold for eight years. It has successfully claimed the affection of many children and adults alike.

Brooks described an organization structure for robots that he calls Subsumption Architecture. His theory is based on the evolutionary development of the human brain. In our brains at least three different levels or parts appear to exist[122]. The most primitive part takes care of basic life support activities such as breathing and blood pressure. The second part, which Vroon[123] calls the reptile brain, takes care of primary behavior such as sleeping, eating and procreation. The part that has developed last, the neocortex, is responsible for complex activities such as science and contemplation about our existence. These three parts act somewhat independently of each other. The neocortex may be very aware for example that smoking is bad for you, but the reptile brain craves instant satisfaction that may still result in you smoking. Or not, depending on which part of your brain, or in this context: which behavior can override the other. That means that at any given moment dozens of different behaviors may be active in your brain. They all interact and that results in your actual conduct.

Back to Brooks' theory. Subsumption literally means:

"To subsume, meaning to classify, include, or incorporate in a more comprehensive category or under a general principle."

So subsumption basically means to organize, re-organize, within the robot different behaviors that exist at any given time, and interact with each other. Depending on the

---

[118] Brooks, R.A., A robust layered control mechanism for mobile robots, AI memo 864, Massachusetts Institute of Technology Artificial Intelligence Laboratory, September 1985.

[119] Head, W, A day in the life of Aibo, Personal Computer World. Vol. 23, no. 5, pp. 76-7. May 2000

[120] Kaplan, F., Talking AIBO : First Experimentation of Verbal Interactions with an Autonomous Four-legged Robot, Sony Computer Science Laboratory, Paris, 2000

[121] Artificial Intelligence roBOt, AIBO sounds like the Japanese word for friend or pal.

[122] MacLean, P.D, The Triune Brain in Evolution · Role in Paleocerebral Functions, 1990, ISBN 978-0-306-43168-5

[123] Vroon, P, De tranen van de krokodil, over de snelle evolutie van onze hersenen (The tears of the crocodile, on the fast evolution of our brains), 1989, ISBN10: 9026319770

circumstances the interactions will be different, and the resulting conduct, or action, of the robot will be different too.

Here is an example of how this works in a human brain. Let's say you reach for your soldering iron without actually looking. Accidentally you grab the wrong side, which is of course very hot. Your body will react instantly by releasing the iron and pulling your hand back, often before you even realize something is wrong. If the heat radiation of the iron is large enough your hand will be pulled back even before you touch the iron. So the these two behaviors:

- get an object
- don't touch hot objects

are by default arranged in such a way that you will not grab a hot object.

But suppose you concentrate on what you are doing, and you are committed to grab the hot part. Now you can get your hand very close to the hot iron, and if you really want to you can actually grab it and get burned. The same two behaviors still exist within your brain, but now they are arranged differently, in such a way that you can grab the hot iron.

Your behaviors as such haven't changed, but what has changed is the interrelation, the way they interact with each other. It is this effect, that Brooks is referring to with the word subsumption.

In robots this works the exact same way. An example by Brooks[124] himself. Picture yourself a mobile robot with two different behaviors on board:

- detect objects
- avoid objects

Detect objects means that the robot will stop when an object is too close to it's sensors. Avoid objects means to actively stay away from objects, so to move if needed.

Now suppose an extra behavior is added:

- move towards the wall

---

[124] Brooks, R.A., How to Build Complete Creatures Rather than Isolated Cognitive Simulators, Architectures for Intelligence, 1991

When this behavior is activated for whatever reason the combination of the behaviors "avoid objects" and "move towards the wall" will result in a wall following conduct. The next Figure shows why this is so.

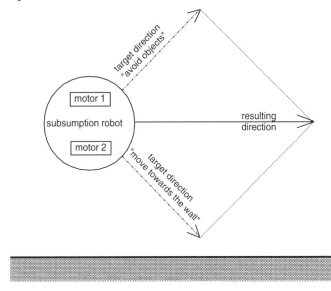

Figure 104. Vector addition of the behaviors.

Both behaviors try to control the robot's motors in an attempt to steer it in a certain direction. These directions can be added together. Mathematicians call this a vector addition. The resulting direction (and speed for that matter) is a vector addition of the different behaviors involved.

	avoid object	move towards the wall	result
motor 1	0	100	100
motor 2	100	0	100

If the behavior "move towards the wall' is de-activated the robot will move away from the wall and stop as soon as the sensors do not detect the wall anymore.

This example is very interesting, because it shows that all behaviors can function independently. That means they can also be developed independently. Only after they are combined in a single robot will they interact. This means extremely complex robots can be designed using relatively simple behavioral building blocks. And that in turn lowers the cost and the development time. This explains why Sony was so eager to use the subsumption technology for the AIBO robot dog.

In the previous example both behaviors are capable of controlling the motors, and the result is a vector addition. There is an alternative mode of operation where one behavior simply blocks the access of another behavior to the motors. Much like in the example of the soldering iron. The "don't touch hot objects" behavior blocked the access to your arm of the "grab an object" behavior, and in fact took over control.

In order to decide which behavior should be allowed to block other behaviors levels have been created. These levels are called competence levels. Competence level zero (or just short: level zero) might contain the following behaviors:

- detect object
- avoid collision

These behaviors could be re-arranged, or subsumptioned if you like, by behaviors on higher levels. For example if they want to collide on purpose, or perhaps just touch something. It is very important to understand that a lower level does NOT mean a lower priority!

Subsumption architecture thus follows these rules:

1. The robot contains multiple behaviors.
2. These behaviors are subdivided into levels, where each level can (and normally will) contain multiple behaviors.
3. Behaviors on lower levels can be rearranged by behaviors on that same or higher levels (subsumption). This can be done by modifying the input (suppression), or by blocking the output (inhibition) of these behaviors, or, as they are often called in the scientific world: state machines[125].
4. The influence of all active behaviors on the propulsion of the robot (usually the motors) is determined by vector addition. If a behavior is inhibited by another behavior then it is no longer part of that addition, even though the behavior itself may be active

---

[125] A state machine is a model of a behavior that consists of a fixed number of situations, called states, and the transition between them.

170

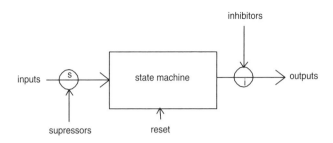

Figure 105. Brooks' state machine[126].

The Figure above shows a behavior, or state machine, graphically. The Reset represents an external signal that activates or de-activates the behavior. This could be a timer (for example the robot gets sleepy after nine hours of operation) or a sensor (for example object approaching forward sensors: back up). It is not meant as a reset in the traditional sense of the word: a button to reset the behavior into an initial situation.

Of course not every one was enthusiastic about Brooks subsumption architecture. The main complaint was that his initial robots were too simple[127], incapable of performing complex tasks and thus not worth to be studied. Brooks response was to build a complex subsumption robot that could collect empty soda can from desks in any office building. And he wrote an article[128] "Elephants don't play chess" where he writes that no-one refuses to study elephants just because they cannot perform complex tasks such as play chess[129].

Subsumption architecture sounds rather complex, and in fact it is. If you want more information on subsumption it is best to limit yourself to scientific articles. Hobby websites rarely contain an accurate representation of Brooks' concepts. Particularly the difference between low level and low priority if often misunderstood.

In the rest of this chapter we will discuss three subsumption robots with increasing complexity. They are based on real robots designed and built by Brooks and Connell. But we will start with one of my robots.

---

[126] Inhibitors and suppressors typically are connected to state machines in higher levels (or not connected at all if higher levels do not exist)

[127] Hartley R, cs, Experiments with the subsumption architecture, Robotics and Automation, 1991. Proceedings., 1991, 1652-1658 vol.2

[128] Brooks, R.A., Elephants don't play chess, Robotics and Autonomous Systems 6 (1990) 3-15.

[129] In Thailand I've seen elephants make paintings, so maybe playing chess is not that far fetched at all.

10.1   The wanderer

The Wanderer[130] is a simple robot that likes sleep and rest. When somebody approaches the Wanderer it gets scared and backs away. Every once in a while it wakes up from its nap, wanders about for a while, and then gets back to sleep again.

The wanderer has four behaviors in two competence levels:

level	behavior
1	Random Walk
0	Obstacle Detect Collision Avoidance Motor Control

When Random Walk becomes active it is simply added to the other two. There is no suppression or inhibition. The final direction in which the robot moves is thus a vector addition of all active behaviors.

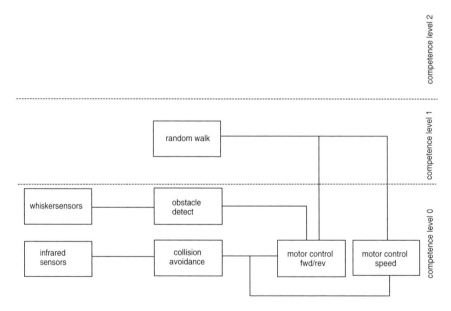

Figure 106. Behaviors and competence levels.

---

[130] Based on the "Wander" robot, van Dam, 1998.

Given the extendibility of the subsumption architecture each behavior must be designed in such a way that new behaviors can be added without modifying the existing ones. That means that Random Walk has the handles for inhibition or suppression already in its code, even though it is currently the highest level behavior present in the robot. This requires the use of many different variables, so a uniform naming system is required to keep it understandable for the human programmer.

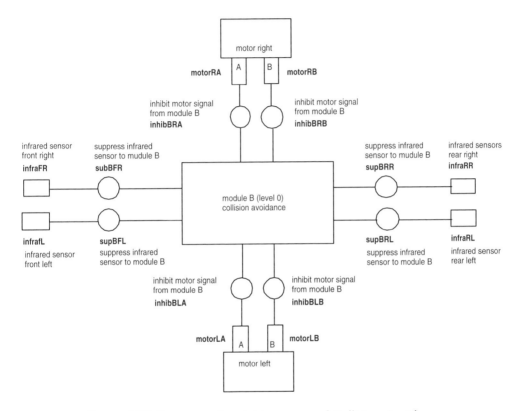

Figure 107. Sensor and variable names of Collision Avoidance.

The previous Figure, which shows the Collision Avoidance behavior as an example, looks more complicated than it really is. Every behavior is assigned a letter. For Collision Avoidance this is the letter B.

All sensors are coded based on their function and location on the robot. An infrared detector mounted on the front of the robot on the right hand side is called infraFR from infrared Front Right.

The possibility to suppress is coded after the name of the behavior and the location of the sensor that needs to be suppressed. For example the variable that can suppress the signal

173

from the sensor on the front right hand side to behavior B is called supBFL (suppress behavior B Front Left sensor.

The variable that inhibits the signal of a behavior to a motor is named after the behavior, the side of the motor and the actual motor contact. So for example the variable that inhibits the connection of behavior B to contact A of the motor on the right hand side is called inhibBLA: inhibit behavior B motor Left contact A.

Essential for the subsumption architecture is that these inhibition and suppression variables are used by behaviors on a higher (or the same) competence level. So for example the variables supBFL and inhibBLA will be used by behaviors in levels 0 or higher to control the Collision Avoidance behavior.

All behaviors of the Wanderer can directly control the motors. That means the signals will be vector added using the OR operator. The consequence of this is that none of the behaviors is capable of stopping the motors if one of the others wants to move. That means that direction "true" must be reverse (driving backwards), because that is the only way that Collision Avoidance can do it's work.

If for example Collision Avoidance and Random Walk both control the motors the following table applies.

Random Walk	Collision Avoidance	Movement of the robot
false (forward)	false(forward)	forward
false (forward)	true(reverse)	reverse
true (reverse)	false(forward)	reverse
true(reverse)	true(reverse)	reverse

So if Collision Avoidance kicks in (sends a 'true" to the motor), the only possible direction for the robot is reverse (or stop).

Every motor has two signals, one for the direction (D) and one for the speed (S). A similar coding system to the sensors will be used, so motorRD for example stands for **motor R**ight **D**rive. The S and D signals have the following influence on the motors:

	reverse	stop	forward	stop
D (direction)	true	true	false	false
S (speed)	true	false	true	false

174

The Random Walk behavior is active for a short period of time only. The rest of the time the robot is inactive (assuming nobody gets too close). The chance that the robot starts a walk is (255-200)/255 = 22%. This chance is the "reset" that Brooks was talking about in the "state machine" Figure.

A walk in progress has a 20/255 = 8% chance to stop again. The net effect is that the Random Walk periods are relatively short. If you want to lengthen the walking time simply modify the chances. The chance to make a turn by the way is also 22%.

This is the Random Walk behavior in JAL.

```
-- ---------------------------------------------------------------------
-- module 1-A (level 1): random walk
-- ---------------------------------------------------------------------
RandomVal = random_byte
if randomval > 200 | walking == true then
   walking = true
   if ! inhibWRD then motorRD = motorRD | false end if   -- forward direction
   if ! inhibWLD then motorLD = motorLD | false end if
   if ! inhibWRS then motorRS = motorRS | true end if      -- in a straight line
   if ! inhibWLS then motorLS = motorLS | true end if
   RandomVal = random_byte                         -- or perhaps a turn instead
   if randomval > 200 then
      if ! inhibWRS then motorRS = motorRS | false end if
      if ! inhibWRD then motorRD = motorRD | false end if
   end if
   if randomval < 50 then
      if ! inhibWLS then motorLS = motorLS | false end if
      if ! inhibWLD then motorLD = motorLD | false end if
   end if
   RandomVal = random_byte
   if randomval < 20 then
      walking = false
   end if
end if
```

You will recognize the inhibWRD variable which higher (or same) level behaviors can use to block Random Walks access to the motors.

There are two interesting behaviors in level zero. The simplest one is Obstacle Detect. This behavior gets its information from the two metal whiskers at the front of the robot.

During normal operation these should never be engaged[131], it is the final safeguard against damaging the robot. For security reasons inhibiting or suppressing this behavior is impossible. As soon as the whiskers are hit the robot can no longer move forward. A higher level behavior will be required to back the robot up (if not it will stay there forever).

```
-- ---------------------------------------------------------------------
-- module 0-B (level 0): obstacle detect (halt immediately)
-- ---------------------------------------------------------------------
if feelFR | feelFL then
        motorRD = true
        motorLD = true
end if
```

The other level zero behavior is Collision Avoidance. This behavior uses four infrared sensors on the four "corners" of the robot. As long as these sensors are clear the behavior is inactive. An object detected by sensors will activate the behavior. It will try to move the robot away from the object that it has detected. Note that the infrared sensors because of their design give a reversed signal, so "true" means that everything is clear.

```
-- ---------------------------------------------------------------------
-- module 0-C (level 0): collision avoidance (move away from obstacles)
-- ---------------------------------------------------------------------
if infraFR & ! supBFR then
    -- right front infrared turn left backwards
    if ! inhibBRD then motorRD = motorRD | false end if  -- stop
    if ! inhibBRS then motorRS = motorRS | false end if
    if ! inhibBLD then motorLD = motorLD | true end if   -- reverse
    if ! inhibBLS then motorLS = motorLS | true end if
end if

if infraFL & ! supBFL then
    -- left front infrared turn right backwards
    if ! inhibBRD then motorRD = motorRD | true end if   -- reverse
    if ! inhibBRS then motorRS = motorRS | true end if
    if ! inhibBLD then motorLD = motorLD | false end if  -- stop
    if ! inhibBLS then motorLS = motorLS | false end if
end if
```

---

[131] In reality it may happen because the robot is rather wide for just two sensors. Besides higher level behavior might decide that the robot needs to touch something, which would also engage the whiskers.

```
if infraRR & ! supBRR then
    -- right rear infrared turn right forward
    if ! inhibBRD then motorRD = motorRD | false end if   -- forward
    if ! inhibBRS then motorRS = motorRS | true end if
    if ! inhibBLD then motorLD = motorLD | false end if   -- stop
    if ! inhibBLS then motorLS = motorLS | false end if
end if

if infraRL & ! supBRL then
    -- left rear infrared turn left forward
    if ! inhibBRD then motorRD = motorRD | false end if   -- stop
    if ! inhibBRS then motorRS = motorRS | false end if
    if ! inhibBLD then motorLD = motorLD | false end if   -- forward
    if ! inhibBLS then motorLS = motorLS | true end if
end if
```

The rest of the program consists of a few pages of sensor readings, motor control, declarations, initializations et cetera. We will not discuss that here. If you want you can read the source code, it is commented at strategic positions. For each behavior you will also find an overview of all variables in use by this behavior. This is very convenient in case you want to add your own behaviors to this robot. In principle you can add as many behavior as you like!

Hardware

The schematic and the picture can be used to build the hardware. You need to build a robot frame, battery pack and the control electronics first. You will find the instructions in the appendix.

In this project the GP2Y0D340K infrared object detector is used. Infrared light is invisible to humans, and just as normal light objects reflect it. By measuring the amount of reflected light one can determine if an object is within range.

The obvious disadvantage is that objects that reflect infrared better appear to be closer than they are in reality. This sensor can spot a black object at 9 inches, but a white object at 23 inches! The sensor causes a lot of disruptions on the power lines due to the "long" wires. A 1000 uF capacitor per two sensors can fix that

In total the robot carries these sensors:

Sensor	Quantity
Infrared	4 x Sharp GP2Y0D340K infrared object detectors
Mechanical	2 x metal whiskers

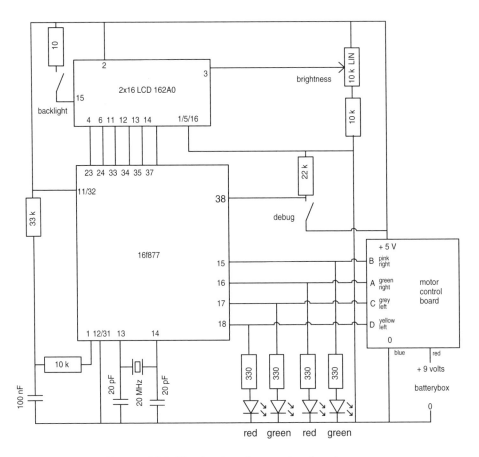

Figure 108. The basic subsumption hardware.

The hardware schematic is split in two parts for easier reading. The first part contains the microcontroller, the LCD display, LEDs to indicate the motor power and a debug switch. This switch can prevent the motors from engaging. That means you can debug the robot without it speeding away off your desk.

The second part contains the sensor arrays. The numbers in the schematic refer to the pin numbers of the microcontroller where these wires have to be connected to. The letters indicate where the sensor must be mounted: F = front, R = rear, L = left and R is right.

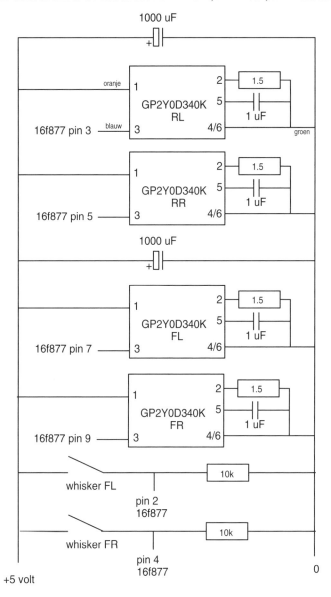

Figure 109. Additional hardware for the Wanderer.

The next Figure shows what the Wanderer looks like in reality. The four infrared sensors have been rotated slightly outwards. The proper adjustment is rather difficult because the robot is a bit wide and the range of the sensors is a bit narrow. In the ideal situation you would have 8 sensors all around. The number of pins on our microcontroller is limited (we will need more pins for the robots in the next projects), and the power consumption would be high for the small AA batteries that we use.

Figure 110. The Wanderer is operational.

The whiskers consist of a thin bare metal wire through a coil of a second bare metal wire. If something touches the whisker the wires make contact thus closing the circuit to the microcontroller.

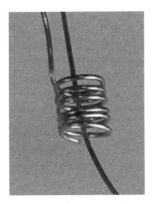

Figure 111. Detail picture of a whisker.

Instructions

Put the robot on a large flat surface (such as the floor) and switch it on. If you approach the robot it will back up, otherwise nothing happens until Random Walk kicks in and the robot starts driving around.

During operation the Wanderer emits a debug signal that can be shown on the PC using the pass-through functionality of the Wisp programmer. The debug signal consists of these data:

```
-- ----------------------------------------------------------------------
-- Report: send data to the PC for evaluation during debugging
-- ----------------------------------------------------------------------

dPC0 = infraFR
dPC1 = infraFL
dPC2 = infraRR
dPC3 = infraRL
dPC4 = pin_b5
dPC5 = feelFR
dPC6 = feelFL
dPC7 = true
serial_sw_write(debugPC)
```

You can visualize this using MICterm , where *dPC0* is bit zero of *debugPC*, *dPC1* is bit one et cetera.

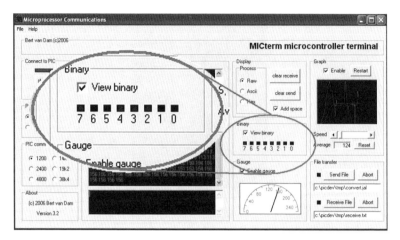

Figure 112. Debugging of the Wanderer using MICterm.

By flipping the debug switch you can disengage the motors. Note that you need quite a bit of clearance around the robot for debugging otherwise the infrared sensors might spot you.

Optional 1

The Random Walk behavior is active for short periods of time only. You can make the robot more active by changing this.

Optional 2

The Random Walk behavior has no purpose, it is, well, random. It is possible to have the robot make certain figures such as a heart. You could program a new behavior and call this "The Painter". By mounting a small pen underneath the robot and lowering it when the behavior starts you can give your floor a whole new design. If you leave the Random Walk behavior also in the robot (inhibited by The Painter!) the hearts will be drawn at different places. Note that any object in the path of the robot will make it deflect which will have a negative influence on the heart, if it happens to be drawing one at the time.

Before doing this you may want to check if the pen you use can be removed from the floor. It's amazing how permanent non-permanent markers are on a parquet floor...

10.2   The Space Lover

The Space Lover[132] just loves open spaces. Just like the wander it likes to nap or wander about for a bit, but in its heart it loves the freedom of open space. On a regular basis it tries to get as far away as possible from walls and other obstacles.

The next Figure shows the path of the Space Lover during one of its trips through my house.[133] Starting in my office at the X it felt the need for an open space and moved towards the living room. The strange movements in the circle are caused by me taking pictures. Apparently it didn't quite like me getting too close to the sensors. The route continues into the kitchen where it almost gets stuck between a kitchen cabinet and the waste basket. It takes a bit of time to escape and it repeatedly switches between it's different behaviors. Eventually it manages to get away and disappears into the corridor

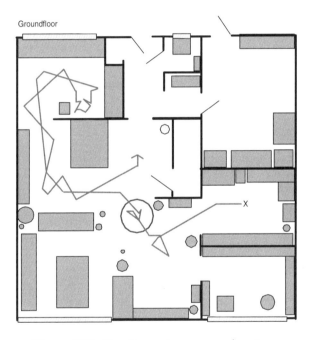

Figure 113. The Space Lover on adventure.

The subsumption architecture of the Space Lover consists of an extra competence level (2) added to the Wanderer. This level consists of a single behavior: Go For Open Spaces.

---

[132] Based on the "Alan" robot, Brooks, 1986
[133] Space Lover had a different frame but the same hardware electronics and subsumption software.

183

This behavior has access to ultrasonic[134] long range sensors and has the capability to suppress the infrared sensor readings to the Collision Avoidance behavior[135] in such a way that objects can be approached closer than Collision Avoidance would normally permit. Go For Open Spaces doesn't attempt to avoid collisions, it leaves that entirely up to Collision Avoidance, it just supplies the behavior with different range data. Which by the nature of these sensors (ultrasonic versus infrared) are much more accurate.

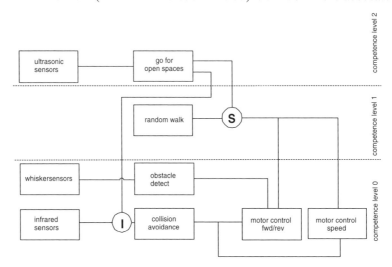

Figure 114. Subsumption architecture of the Space Lover.

The behaviors in this robot can be arranged in three different ways, which cause a totally different conduct.

---

[134] Ultrasonic sensors emit ultrasonic sound, and measure the time it takes for this sound to bounce back off an object. From this time the distance can be calculated. More information on this subject can be found in the book PIC microcontrollers, 50 projects for beginners and experts, Elektor ISBN 978-0-905705-70-5, page 156.
[135] Just the measurement of the infrared sensors at the front because there are no ultrasonic sensors at the rear of the robot.

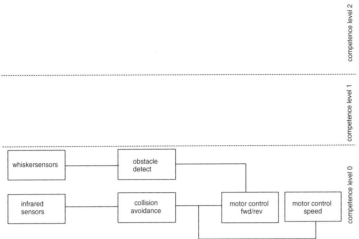

Figure 115. Level zero competence.

Quietly sleeping, runs away when someone gets too close. Level 0 competence: guarding the safety of the robot.

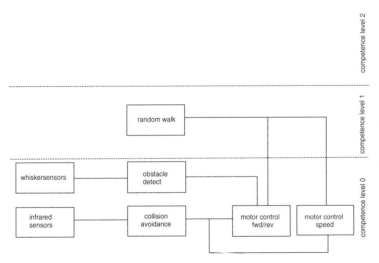

Figure 116. Level one competence.

Wandering about without worrying where to, in fact without even bothering to look. Trusts on level 0 behavior to prevent accidents. A kind of Carpe Diem conduct.

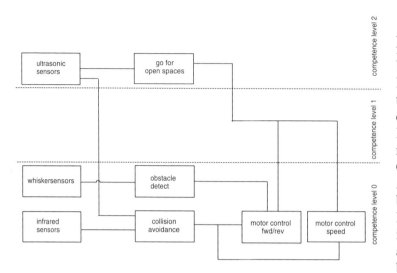

competence level 2
competence level 1
competence level 0

Figure 117. Level 2 competence.

Actively looking for open spaces. Uses ultrasonic long range sensors to scan the environment. Relays these readings to the Collision Avoidance behavior two levels lower to increase the accuracy of this behavior without affecting its decision making process.

When Go For Open Spaces engages it will suppress the Random Walk behavior. So even if this behavior kicks in, it will not have an effect on the robot. Then the robot starts moving. In principle in a straight line, but the robot will turn towards the sensor that measures the largest distance. The maximum distance the sensors can measure is about 70 feet, so larger spaces all look alike to the Space Lover.

There is no direct variable with which the Space Lover can change the infrared sensor readings used by the Collision Avoidance behavior, only one to completely suppress the signal. So this behavior modifies the infrared sensor readings before the are received by Collision Avoidance.

The Go For Open Spaces behavior looks like this in JAL:

```
-- ------------------------------------------------------------------------
-- module 2-A (level 2): look for wide open space
-- ------------------------------------------------------------------------

RandomVal = random_byte
if randomval > 180 | space == true then
   space = true
```

```
-- inhibit wander behavior
inhibWRD = true
inhibWRS = true
inhibWLD = true
inhibWLS = true

-- move straight ahead
if ! inhibSRD then motorRD = motorRD | false end if
if ! inhibSLD then motorLD = motorLD | false end if
if ! inhibSRS then motorRS = motorRS | true end if
if ! inhibSLS then motorLS = motorLS | true end if

-- unless the open space is...
if rangeR > rangeL & rangeR > rangeM then
  -- ... to the right, so turn right
  if ! inhibSRS then motorRS = motorRS | true end if
  if ! inhibSRD then motorRD = motorRD | true end if
end if

if rangeL > rangeR & rangeL > rangeM then
  -- ... to the left, so turn left
  if ! inhibSLS then motorLS = motorLS | true end if
  if ! inhibSLD then motorLD = motorLD | true end if
end if

--Suppression of the obstacle avoidance front inputs is possible
-- using suppression bits. We want this behavior to use ultrasonic data
-- instead however, and that cannot be done using the suppression bits.
-- So we simply tamper with the infrared sensor readings, and
-- make the obstacle avoidance module non the wiser!

if rangeR < 5 then
   infraFR = true
else
   infraFR = false
end if
if rangeL < 5 then
   infraFL = true
else
   infraFL= false
end if
```

```
-- see if it's time to quit
RandomVal = random_byte
if randomval < 20 then
   space = false
end if
end if
```

As you can see the Go For Open Spaces behavior is simply added to the existing robot software, without making any changes what so ever! In his famous memo Brooks[136] writes:

" The key idea of levels of competence is that we can build layers of a control system corresponding to each level of competence and simply add a new layer to an existing set to move to the next higher level of overall competence. We start by building a complete robot control system that achieves level 0 competence. It is debugged thoroughly. We never alter that system. We call it the zeroth-level control system. Next we build another control layer, which we call the first-level control system. It is able to examine data from the level 0 system and is also permitted to inject data into the internal interfaces of level 0 suppressing the normal data flow. This layer, with the aid of the zeroth, achieves level 1 competence. The zeroth layer continues to run unaware of the layer above it, which sometimes interferes with its data paths. The same process is repeated to achieve higher levels of competence. We call this architecture a subsumption architecture."

Brooks identifies a total of eight competence levels. In this book we will not proceed past level two because level three requires location determination equipment (such as a GPS system) which our robot doesn't have.

---

[136] Brooks, R.A., A robust layered control mechanism for mobile robots, AI memo 864, Massachusetts Institute of Technology Artificial Intelligence Laboratory, September 1985.

competence level	description
0	Avoid contact with stationary or moving objects.
1	Wander aimlessly without hitting anything.
2	Explore the world, by seeing places far away but reachable, and going there.
3	Map the environment, and plan routes from one place to another.
4	Notice changes in the (static) environment.
5	Discriminate between different objects, and perform actions with these objects.
6	Formulate plans and execute them, thereby modifying the environment in a favorable way (for the robot)
7	Gain insight in the behavior and function of objects in the world, and adapt your plans accordingly.

Hardware

You can use the schematic and the picture to built the hardware. Of course you first need to build a robot frame with control electronics and a battery pack. Then you need to add all the hardware shown in the Wanderer project. Add to that the schematic shown in this project. You see that the robot grows in complexity, both hardware and software, as we go along. Each additional behavior however is not complex at all, and easy to add.

In total the robot is now equipped with the following sensors:

Sensor	Quantity
Infrared	4 x Sharp GP2Y0D340K infrared object detectors
Mechanical	2 x metal whiskers
Ultrasonic	3 x Devantech SRF04 Ultrasonic Range Finders

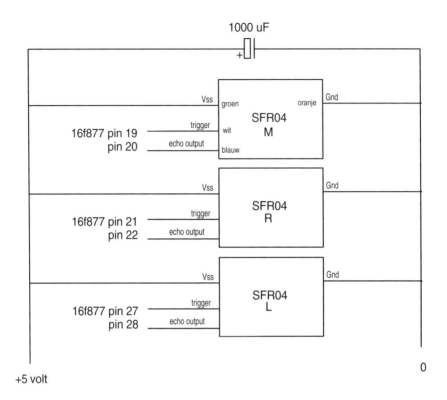

Figure 118. Additional hardware for the Space Lover.

Figure 119. The Space Lover operational.

On the picture the voltage stabilizer UA7805 doesn't have a heat sink. Strictly speaking that is not a problem, but it does get rather hot. If you want to use the robot for extended periods of time perhaps it is best to mount a small heat sink. A U shaped metal sink of about one square inch should be enough. Of course you can also screw the UA7805 directly to the metal base of the robot.

Instructions

Put the robot on the floor and switch it on. Which behavior will kick in first, or in fact what it will do at any point of time, is totally unpredictable. In practice it will not take long for something to happen.

The Space Lover generates a debug signal that can be visualized on the PC using the pass-through functionality of the Wisp programmer.

```
-- ------------------------------------------------------------------------
-- Report: send data to the PC for evaluation during debugging
-- ------------------------------------------------------------------------

    dPC0 = infraFR
    dPC1 = infraFL
    dPC2 = infraRR
    dPC3 = infraRL
    dPC4 = pin_b5
    dPC5 = feelFR
    dPC6 = feelFL
    dPC7 = true

    serial_sw_write(debugPC)
```

Optional

The Space Lover has sufficient sensors on board to find it's way out of mazes. Most used is the "left hand against the wall" method, which ensures that you will always find an exit from any entrance (though maybe not the exit you had in mind).

10.3   The Hunter

The Hunter[137] is the most playful robot of the three subsumption robots. It likes to play with humans or animals by following them around, or even hunting them. This behavior is not controlled by timers but by the ultrasonic sensors. When an object is within 'hunting range' the Hunter will chase it, while maintaining a safe distance. When the prey stops moving the hunter will wait for it to start moving again. After a while hunting starts to bore him and other behaviors can take control.

---

[137] Based on the "Tom" robot, Connell, 1987

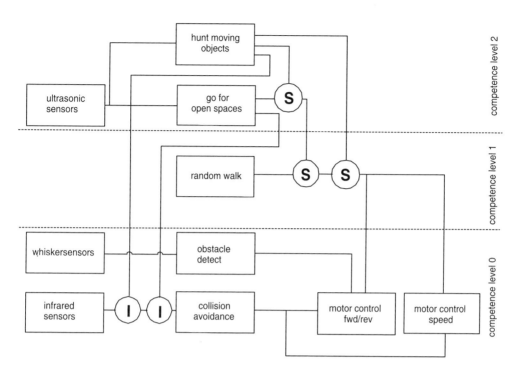

Figure 120, The subsumption architecture of the Hunter.

Hunt Moving Objects will suppress Go For Open Spaces and Random Walk. Note that these behaviors can become active, but they have no influence on the motors as long as Hunt Moving Objects is active. Hunt Moving Objects inhibits the connection between the forward infrared sensors and Collision Avoidance. This is required because during the hunt the robot needs to be able to get much closer than Collision Avoidance would ever allow. Hunt Moving Objects takes care of avoiding collisions at the front of the robot using the ultrasonic sensors. At the rear Collision Avoidance is still in control.

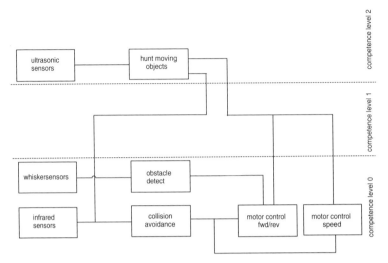

competence level 2

competence level 1

competence level 0

Actively follows moving objects. Uses ultrasonic sensors to scan the environment. Blocks the forward facing infrared sensors and uses ultrasonic sensors to avoid collisions, while Collision Avoidance is in control of the rear infrared sensors.

Figure 121. Level 2 competence

The JAL software that takes care of this behavior is added to the software of the Space Lover without any modifications. Just the *inhibHxx* variables have been added to the debug switch. It is fascinating to see how such a tiny addition can have such a huge impact on the conduct of the robot. Subsumption truly is an amazing technology.

In JAL the Hunt Moving Objects behavior looks like this:

```
-- ---------------------------------------------------------------------------
-- module 2-B (level 2): hunter
-- ---------------------------------------------------------------------------
hunter = false
hundir = 0

if rangeL < 70 then
    hunter = true
    hundir = 1
end if

if rangeR < 70 then
    hunter = true
    hundir = 3
end if
```

```
if rangeM < 70  then
    hunter = true
    hundir = 2
end if

if hunter == true & huntcounter > 20 then

    -- inhibit wander behavior
    inhibWRD = true
    inhibWRS = true
    inhibWLD = true
    inhibWLS = true

    -- inhibit open space behavior
    inhibSRD = true
    inhibSRS = true
    inhibSLD = true
    inhibSLS = true

    -- inhibit obstacle detect front sensors
    supBFR = true
    supBFL = true

    -- move in appropriate direction
    -- straight ahead
    if hundir == 2 then
        if ! inhibHRD then motorRD = motorRD | false end if
        if ! inhibHRS then motorRS = motorRS | true end if
        if ! inhibHLD then motorLD = motorLD | false end if
        if ! inhibHLS then motorLS = motorLS | true end if
    end if

    if hundir == 3 then
        -- turn right
        if ! inhibHRS then motorRS = motorRS | truc end if
        if ! inhibHRD then motorRD = motorRD | true end if
        if ! inhibHLS then motorLS = motorLS | true end if
        if ! inhibHLD then motorLD = motorLD | false end if
    end if
```

```
if hundir == 1 then
    -- turn left
    if ! inhibHRS then motorRS = motorRS | true end if
    if ! inhibHRD then motorRD = motorRD | false end if
    if ! inhibHLS then motorLS = motorLS | true end if
    if ! inhibHLD then motorLD = motorLD | true end if
end if

-- if right in front of hunted object
if rangeM < 15 then
    -- stop motors
    if ! inhibHLS then motorLS = false end if
    if ! inhibHRS then motorRS = false end if
end if

else
    hunter = false
end if

huntcounter = huntcounter + 1
if huntcounter > 100 then huntcounter = 0 end if
```

The Hunter will continue hunting (or waiting) as long as *huntcounter* is between 20 and 100. Since one single program loop takes roughly 0.4 seconds the following table applies.

huntcounter		behavior	time
start	**end**		
0	20	Everything except Hunt Moving Objects	8 sec
20	100	Hunt Moving Objects	32 sec
N/A	N/A	All behaviors	no limit

If you want the hunter to play longer increase the maximum *huntcounter* to a value higher than 100.

Hardware

This robot uses the exact same hardware as the Space Lover. So in affect it carries these sensors:

Sensor	Quantity
Infrared	4 x Sharp GP2Y0D340K infrared object detectors
Mechanical	2 x metal whiskers
Ultrasonic	3 x Devantech SRF04 Ultrasonic Range Finders

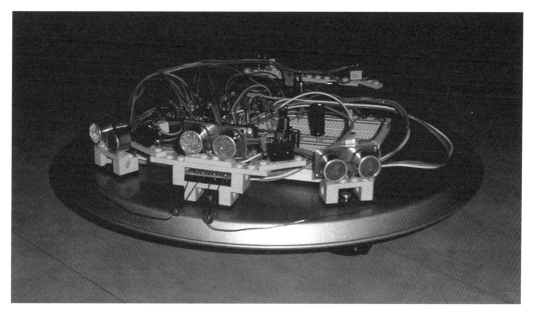

Figure 122. The hunter searching for prey.

Instructions

Put the robot on the floor and switch it on. To get the hunter to actually hunt an object it should be within hunting range, which means less than 18 inch[138] away from the front of the robot. It will then turn towards the object and chase after it. As long as the distance is smaller than 18 inch the hunter will keep chasing the object. If the Hunter gets to within about five inch it will stop (the prey has been "caught") and wait. After about half a

---

[138] The reading has to be less than 70, which is about equivalent to 18 inch.

minute the Hunter will get bored and start to do something else. For a short while it will then refuse to play, being annoyed because the prey didn't move any more.

The Hunter generates a debug signal that can be visualized on the PC using the pass-through functionality of the Wisp programmer.

```
-- ------------------------------------------------------------------------
-- Report: send data to the PC for evaluation during debugging
-- ------------------------------------------------------------------------
```

```
dPC0 = infraFR
dPC1 = infraFL
dPC2 = infraRR
dPC3 = infraRL
dPC4 = pin_b5
dPC5 = feelFR
dPC6 = feelFL
dPC7 = true

serial_sw_write(debugPC)
```

On the LCD you can see which behaviors are active, though that doesn't necessarily mean they are actually in control of the robot. A behavior doesn't know if it is being suppressed or inhibited by another behavior. So you could for example see both an H and a W on the display, where only the H (The Hunter) is in control.

Optional 1

The Hunt Moving Objects is very controlling because it kicks in every time an object gets close. A fun modification might be to add an LDR and allow Hunt Moving Objects only in the dark. Note that at the moment all analog pins are switched to digital by the JAL program.

Optional 2

By adding sensors that allow location measurements (such as GPS) or wheel sensors that allow dead reckoning[139]) behaviors on competence level three might be added to the robot. The result could be that the robot returns to a fixed point regularly, for example to "drink", like a thirsty animal. So the behavior could be Get A Drink. Note that due to

---

[139] Roston, GP, cs, Dead Reckoning Navigation for Walking Robots, The Robotics Institute, Carnegie Mellon University, Pittsburgh, Pennsylvania, 1991

slippage of the wheels or tractor feeds dead reckoning is not very accurate (nor is GPS on the very short range for that matter) so for the final part of the navigation you may want to rely on the ultrasonic sensors.

Optional 3

Another application for wheel sensors or GPS may be to have to robot store a simple map of the surroundings. Slippage problems and inaccuracy of the sensors makes this a very challenging task!

11 Miscellaneous

This chapter contains projects that don't fit in the mainstream categories.

11.1 Robot with free will

A fruit fly is a 1/8 inch small fly with surprisingly large red eyes. The animal lives off rotting fruit and it very popular with scientist because it's easy to keep in large quantities and the genome (the four chromosomes) is completely known. Many years ago it was even used in high schools for cross breeding and evolutionary experiments.

In may 2007 Maye[140] wrote an article in which he suggested that a fruit fly (Drosophila Melanogaster) could possibly have a free will: *"...suggesting a general neural mechanism underlying spontaneous behavior"*.

The international press jumped all over this, removed all question marks and doubts and claimed in big headlines that fruit flies do have a free will[141].

Figure 123. Fruit fly, photo André Karwath[142].

So what is a free will? The basic concept is that humans and animals respond to external stimuli . How they respond has an element of predictability. If you get cold you put on a sweater, a coat, or you turn up the heat. What you choose depends on the circumstances. If you get cold outdoors a coat would be a logical choice, if you get cold indoors and all you are wearing is a T-shirt then a sweater would probably be a good idea.

---

[140] Maye, A.; Hsieh, C.; Sugihara, G. and Brembs, B. (2007): Order in spontaneous behavior. PLoS One, May 16. DOI number: 10.1371/journal.pone.0000443
[141] Dagblad De Pers (The Netherlands) "Ook een fruitvliegje heeft een eigen willetje", Scientific American (United States) "Defending free will: A fruit fly makes choices", Deutchlandfunk (Germany) "Forscher entdecken, dass Fruchtfliegen zu spontanen Entscheidungen fähig sind".
[142] This picture is licensed under the Creative Commons Attribution ShareAlike 2.5

Sometimes people do things that seem unrelated to any stimuli at all. For example you always go to Spain on your vacation, but this time for no apparent reason you decide to go to Italy instead. The fact that there is no apparent reason, so it looks spontaneous, doesn't mean that there actually is no reason. It just means you are not aware of one. You "simply" decided you want to go to Italy.

Maye places his fruit flies in an environment without any stimuli[143], and observed their behavior. It seems likely that the fruit flies would want to search for food, or a mating partner, but since there were no stimuli, there should be no preferred direction of flight. His expectation was therefor that the movements that the fruit flies made would be completely random.

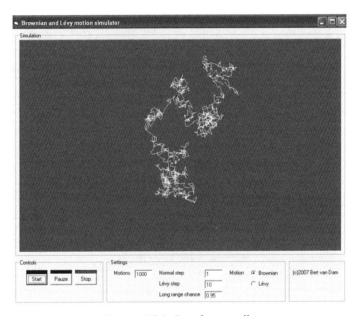

Figure 124. Random walk.

This kind of movement is called "random walk", or Brownian movement, named after scientist Brown[144]. He discovered this motion in molecules that move in a certain random way, influenced by temperature.

---

[143] An empty white space would be without stimuli for humans. If the same is true for fruit flies remains to be seen.

[144] Brown, A Brief Account of Microscopical Observations Made in the Months of June, July, and August, 1827, on the Particles Contained in the Pollen of Plants; and on the General Existence of Active Molecules in Organic and Inorganic Bodies, Edinburgh New Philosophical Journal, Vol. 5, April to September, 1828, pp. 358-371.

The formula for this way of moving is[145]:

$$variance = constant * time$$

Variance is the distance that the fruit fly is, on average, removed from the starting point at a given time. Time and variance grow equally fast: if you wait twice as long the average distance from the starting point will also be twice as large. What this means is that all steps are more or less the same size and go in a random direction.

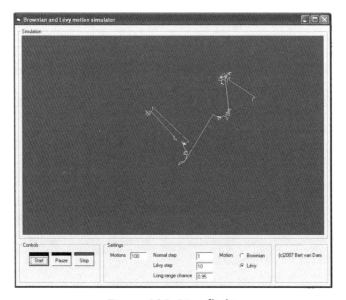

Figure 125. Lévy flight.

In this experiments he observed something else instead.

> *"Instead of random noise, we find a fractal order (resembling Lévy flights) in the temporal structure of spontaneous flight maneuvers in tethered Drosophila fruit flies. Lévy-like probabilistic behavior patterns are evolutionarily conserved, suggesting a general neural mechanism underlying spontaneous behavior."*

Lévy flight is a pattern where small movements are mixed with relatively large movements. The pattern was discovered by the French mathematician Lévy[146].

---

[145] Weeks, ER. cs. Random walks and Levy flights observed in fluid flows, Nonlinear Science Today , Springer-Verlag, 1998

[146] Lévy , P., Théorie de l'Addition des Variables Aléatoires, Gauthier-Villars, Paris, 1937

This pattern is very common in the behavior of foraging animals, such as bees[147]. They forage in the same (small) area for a while until the food is more or less depleted, then they fly a long way away and start searching there again. This is a very efficient search technique[148], which makes sure one doesn't waste too much time in non-productive areas. People use this same technique. When you are shopping for shoes you search in a shoe store, when you don't find something you like you drive to another shoe store and search there. In between you don't waste time searching (unless you are a hobo).

The variance now follows a completely different formula:

$$variance = time^{factor}$$

Where the factor is between 1 and 2. The average distance to the starting point grows much faster then when a random walk is used.

The odd thing is that this behavior took place in a completely stimuli free environment, so the fruit flies had no reason to follow this pattern. There was no signal to start, and there was no signal to abandon the search and fly the long haul to the next location. It is possible that the wiring in the fruit flies brain forces it to fly this pattern no matter what, but it is also possible that this is indeed a sign of free will.

In this project we will build a robot that behaves like a fruit fly. To avoid a philosophical discussion on free will we assume the same position as in the tutorial: if our robot behaves like a creature with free will, than it has free will.

Software

The Visual Basic program that was used to make the previous Figures is part of the software download. In the settings area you can enter the number of steps you want the program to make and what kind of movement you would like to see.

To simulate a Lévy flight in a robot a direction, and the distance to move into that direction, need to be chosen. In JAL the robot library that was made for the genetic algorithm programs can be used. In that library the specifics of our robot, such as turn time and forward speed, have already been taken into account which makes this project a lot easier. The first step is to randomly pick a direction, and see if turning left or right is quickest:

---

[147] Reynolds, AM, Cooperative random Lévy flight searches and the flight patterns of honeybees, Physics Letters A, Volume 354, Issues 5-6, 12 June 2006, Pages 384-388
[148] Bartumeus F, cs, Animal Search Strategies: A Quantitative Random Walk Analyses, Ecology, Vol 86 issue 11 (nov 2005), pp. 3078–3087

```
-- select random number and convert
degrees = random_word/182

-- make the shortest turn
if degrees <= 180 then
    -- turn right
    turn = degrees
    B03(turn)
end if
if degrees > 180 then
    -- turn left
    turn = degrees - 180
    B04(turn)
end if
```

The distance to be moved is usually short, but occasionally long. In a robot 95% short distances and only 5% long distances yield a nice result.

```
-- select a random length
distance = random_byte/12

-- if this is not a Lévy flight reduce to a small step
if random_byte < 242 then distance = 1 + distance/10 end if

B01(distance)
```

So the JAL program uses $255/12 = 21$ cm for the long distance and $21/10 = 2$ cm for the short distance. The ratio 1:10 is equivalent to the patterns made by the Visual Basic "Brownian and Lévy motion simulator". If you prefer a different pattern simply change the numbers in the JAL program. Remember that these variables are defined as bytes so they must be in the range of 0 to 255, and integers only.

Hardware

As hardware you can use the robot of any one of the previous projects. Which one doesn't matter because this project only uses the motors, and those they all have.

Instructions

Put the robot on the floor and switch it on. Make sure there is sufficient space because there is no safeguard against collisions.

Optional

This would be a great pattern of movement for addition to a subsumption robot. In that case you cannot use the robot_bert library because during the waiting loops in this library the robot will not pay attention to the other behaviors. The solution is to work with loop counters just like the Hunt Moving Objects behavior in the Hunter robot. This behavior has a waiting loop to see if the 32 seconds allocated for hunting have already passed. This loop is folded open so to speak, so that the entire program fits inside the loop.

So rather than using a simple 32 second delay, like this:

delay_1s(32)

The Hunt Moving Objects behavior uses a loop counter, like this:

[the program itself (takes 0.4 seconds)]
teller = teller + 1
if teller > 80 then *[done waiting]*
[go back for the next loop]

Every time the program passes this location 0.4 seconds have passed , since in the Hunter subsumption robot one program loops takes 0.4 seconds. So waiting 80 loops takes 80 x 0.4 = 32 seconds. The effect is the same as with delay_1s(32) but the other behaviors (including vital ones such as Collision Avoidance) can remain active.

11.2   Ricochet robot

This chapter doesn't have anything to do with artificial intelligence. It does involve intelligence: yours. This is a game we played while writing this book. It is a lot of fun and not as simple as it looks.

The game principle is based on Ricochet Robots[149] published in 1999. The Ricochet Robots rules are as follows.

The robots on the playing field can move in any direction, but not diagonally. A robot can only stop by running into something, it cannot stop by itself. When a robot is stopped another direction may be chosen. The path that the robot travels between two obstructions is called a move. The object is to get from the starting point to the finish in the least amount of moves.

---

[149] Riogames, www.riograndegames.com/

Figure 126. Ricochet Robots board game[150].

Our version of this game is played with only one robot, and your living room. The robot is equipped with a single ultrasonic sensor at the front, and an infrared photo reflector underneath. When the robot detects an object at 4 inches, it will make a 90 degree turn to the right and continue in that direction. Each turn counts as one point.

The target is a black piece of paper located somewhere in the room. As soon as the sensor underneath the robot detects the black paper it will stop. The object of the game is to hit the target with as many turns (and thus points) as possible. You can choose any starting location you like, and use the furniture in the room as barriers. You may move the furniture, flowerpots or even the cat around as much as you like but once the robot starts moving you cannot change anything anymore.

The more complicated you make your route, the more points you earn. But if the robot misses the target (the black piece of paper) you get no points at all. So you may get more points in the long run using short routes than making long routes.

Hardware

The schematic and the picture can be used to build the hardware. You need to build a robot frame, battery pack and the control electronics first. You will find the instructions in the appendix.

---

[150] Photo: Chris Norwood.

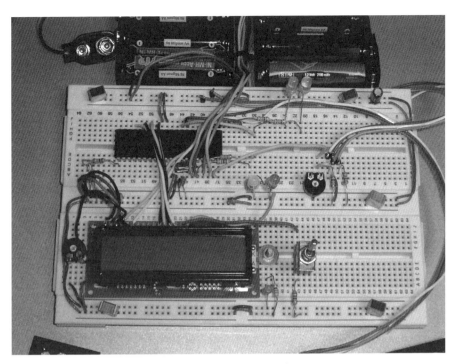

Figure 127. Ricochet robot.

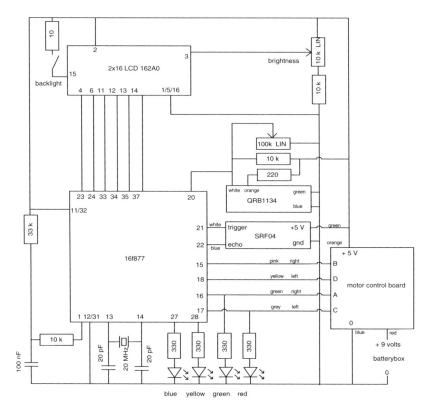

Figure 128. Ricochet robot.

A Fairchild photo reflector is mounted underneath the robot just like in chapter 6.1, and connected to pin 20. If you use a different type of photo reflector then green/orange stands for the connections to the infrared LED, and white/blue for the connections to the infrared transistor. In that case you may need to use different resistors, and a different variable resistor for calibration. Once the hardware is completed download the calibration program into microcontroller:

        -- JAL 2.3
        include 16f877_bert

```
-- define the pins
pin_c0_direction = output      -- motor 1 (left side)
pin_c1_direction = output      -- motor 1 (left side)
pin_c2_direction = output      -- motor 2 (right side)
pin_c3_direction = output      -- motor 2 (right side)
pin_d1_direction = input       -- infrared reflector
pin_d5_direction = output      -- led yellow

-- brake the motors
pin_c1 = 0
pin_c2 = 0
pin_c3 = 0
pin_c4 = 0

forever loop

    -- LED on = black detected
    pin_d5 = pin_d1

end loop
```

Put the robot on top of the black paper that you will use as a target and adjust the 100k variable resistor in such a way that the yellow LED is lit only when the robot is on top of the black paper.

Instructions

Put a black piece of paper somewhere in the living room as target. At each object that the robot detects it will turn 90 degrees to the right. Start simple and place the robot in such a way that it will hit the target after just one turn, just like in the previous Figure. This will help you understand at which distance the robot turns, and how straight (or un-straight) it moves.

Increase the difficulty of the path by incorporating more furniture and thus turns. For each turn you get one point, assuming the robot ends up on the target. If the robot doesn't stop because the sensor missed the target (or the entire robot missed the target) you get zero points.

Figure 129. Will it turn at the right moment and hit the target?

Optional

If the group you play with is large enough you will eventually end up with another rule: all objects may be moved in the wrong direction as long as the person who's turn it is doesn't notice it.

11.3   Menace tic tac toe

In 1960, while working at the University of Edinburgh Michie[151] invented the Machine Educable Noughts And Crosses Engine (MENACE). It is a technique that allows a computer to learn how to play tic tac toe (in the UK called noughts and crosses) that he calls Boxes. It turned the scientific world upside down because it does what everyone thought to be impossible: it made a machine learn. Interestingly enough he didn't have access to a computer powerful enough to run his program so Michie developed and tested it using.... matchboxes.

---

[151] Michie, D., Trial and Error, Science Survey, part 2 pp. 129-45, 1961

Figure 130. Machine learning technique Boxes in action.

Because the playing area of tic-tact-toe consists of only nine fields the number of possible games one can play is manageable[152], namely 255.168. Many of these games are actually identical, only the field is rotated or mirrored (a square has four mirror lines).

Many of the game <u>situations</u> are also identical because it doesn't matter in which order the crosses and zeros were placed on the board. We are only interested in the current situation, not in the history that led up to it. By removing all "identical" game situations only 2.201 remain. And since MENACE always plays cross (and thus starts) only the game situations that cross might encounter in the first four moves are relevant. The fifth and final move is simply filling in the open space. This way only 304 possible game situations remain.

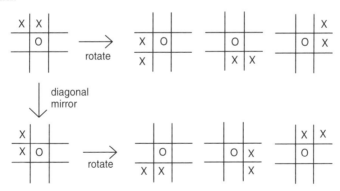

Figure 131. Rotating and mirroring the playing field.

Michie took 304 matchboxes and drew a game situation on each one of them. Every open position in this game situation was assigned a color. For each color a number of beads of the same color was put in the box, according to this table:

---

[152] Henry Bottomley, www.btinternet.com/~se16/hgb/tictactoe.htm

move	number of open positions in the playing field, so this is the number of colors used	number of beads per color
first	9	4
second	7	3
third	5	2
fourth	3	1
fifth	1	-

The next step is to actually play a game. At Michie's turn he would look for the matchbox with the matching game situation. He would shake the box, pick a random bead and put it on top of the box. The box was now placed in a separate row so it was clear which boxes played a roll in this game. The color of the bead told Mitchie where to place his cross.

When Michie (or in fact MENACE) would win, every box with a bead on top would get three extra beads in that color. In the case of a draw one extra bead in that color would be added. In the event of a loss no beads were added, in fact the beads on top were "thrown away".

Interesting about this mechanism that all steps that contributed to the goal are rewarded or punished in the exact same way. So the mechanism doesn't just reward the final move but the strategy as a whole. Quite unlike the technique used in section 2.2.

According to Mitchie a few hundred games were needed to train his machine. That estimate is a bit optimistic, but the result is never the less very impressive. The Stanford University invited Mitchie to the US to program MENACE on an IBM computer. In 1996, looking back, he writes about this time:

> *MENACE was meant as a demonstration of the principles of learning by re-enforcement, as can be seen by the behavior of animals. That it could eventually be used to control a steel mill was an unexpected bonus.*[153]

The program has an excellent, though somewhat slow, learning behavior. It does indeed take a few hundred runs before a significant improvement in game play can be seen. The next Figure shows that the performance of MENACE is stable after some 1500 runs.

---

[153] Controlling a steel mill with BOXES, McGarity, M., Sammut, C., and Clements, D. (1995). In Machine Intelligence 14, pp. 299-322, Oxford: Clarendon Press.

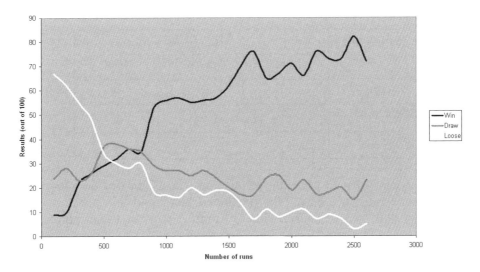

Figure 132. MENACE learning against a player on beginner's level.

The data for this graph have been generated by Adit MENACE, a Visual Basic simulation by Mike Griffiths[154]. In the graph MENACE plays against a player on beginner's level and is gradually becoming an expert. Against an expert player MENACE will eventually draw all the time. Adit is capable of learning automatically, which means that MENACE plays against a built in computer player. Hence the graph with more than 2500 game plays, manually this would have been impossible.

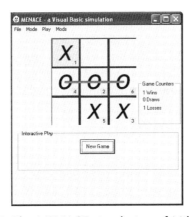

Figure 133. The MENACE simulation of Mike Griffiths.

---

[154] Mike was kind enough to donate the source code for this project, which allowed me to add the microcontroller communications. Credit for the program goes to Mike.

Despite the slow learning speed the results are very impressive. The next table shows the results that MENACE obtained against the computer trainers:

opponent	MENACE		
	win	draw	lose
random	92	3	5
beginner	72	20	8
expert	17	70	13

Tic tac toe is a game that in principle no-one can win. If none of the players makes a mistake the game ends in a draw. The previous table shows that a trained MENACE program doesn't make many mistakes with 70% draws against an expert player.

The interesting part about this technique is that it doesn't contain any rules at all as to how the game should be played! That means the program learns based on the behavior of the opponent. Your own weak spots are ruthlessly exploited by MENACE. Is there a special 'trick' that you always fall for? MENACE will find it and use it over and over again.

In order to convert MENACE to a microcontroller at least 8 kb would be required for storing the game situations and the associated beads. That is not a problem, we could easily add external EEPROM memory. But it is perhaps more interesting to see how our own tic-tac-toe expert program of section 8.1 would perform against a fully trained MENACE program.

Hardware

Build the project of section 8.1 according to the instructions and download the expert program into the microcontroller. Leave the Wisp programmer connected and powered because the pass-through functionality is required for the microcontroller and the PC to communicate with each other.

Instructions

In the download package you will find a modified version of Mike's program, who was kind enough to donate the source code, with as extra the communication to the microcontroller. You now have three choices:

1. Train MENACE using the expert program

This option is the most fun, because MENACE will find any weakness in our expert program and exploit it. If the expert program was set up correctly there are no weaknesses and all games will eventually end in a draw. But is this true?

Take these steps

1. Select File - Initialize.
2. Select Mode - Training.
3. Select Play - Interactive.
4. Click on "Start" (Connect to PIC).
5. Click on "New Game".
6. MENACE now makes a move.
7. Click on "Get PIC move" to get the move from the JAL program.
8. Repeat step 7 (and 6, but that will go automatically) until the game is finished.
9. Return to step 5.

It will take a few hundred games before you see a serious effect, but is easier than it sounds. You don't really have to pay attention: just click on some buttons. I strongly recommend that you at least try this option.

When you are done you can store the training results using File - Save MENACE file, which is a good idea so you don't have to do this twice.

2. Train MENACE personally

This is also fun because now MENACE will find your personal weak spot. The problem is that it takes quite a while and this time you do need to think. Fortunately you can save the results and continue later.

Take these steps:

1. Select File - Initialize.
2. Select Mode - Training.
3. Select Play - Interactive.
4. Click on "New Game".
5. MENACE will now make a move.
6. Click on the field where you want to play your zero.
7. Repeat step 7 (and 6, but that will go automatically) until the game is finished.
8. Return to step 4.

It will take a few hundred games before you see a serious effect.

When you are done you can store the training results using File - Save MENACE file. If you want you can continue training at a later date.

3. Train MENACE automatically

This option is the least fun but it does go rather quickly. A few hundred games can be played in a matter of seconds. The higher the training level the better MENACE will learn to play. This is quit noticeable if you play against a trained program.

Take these steps:

1. Select File - Initialize.
2. Select Mode - Training.
3. Select Play - Automated.
4. Set the number of training games to play.
5. Set the game level of the computer opponent.
6. Set the other settings to your own liking. "Counters only" - "none" - "none" is the setting that leads to the fastest results.
7. Click on "Play".

After the training you can have MENACE play against the JAL Expert program in the same manner as described in option 1.

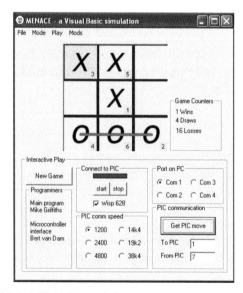

Figure 134. MENACE and the Expert Program showdown.

Optional

If you followed the instructions of option one, or if you let a fully trained MENACE program (on expert level) play against our JAL program you have found the weak spot by now. If not I recommend you try this first, before continuing with this section. Finding it yourself is much more fun!

As discussed in the optional part of section 8.1 the expert program doesn't protect itself against splits made by the opponent. Perhaps you already noticed at that moment that this could cause the expert program to loose. If not then MENACE has noticed it for you and beat the expert program game after game.

These are the steps you need to take to beat the expert program:

1. Cross on 6 (the expert program responds with a zero on 4).
2. Cross on 1 (the expert program responds with a zero on 8).
3. Cross on 0. The field is now split: you can win by placing a cross on 2 or on 3 (in your next move).

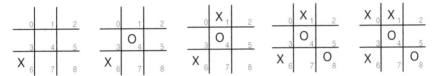

Figure 135. MENACE unveils the weak spot.

To make the expert program invincible you need to add a rule to protect it against splits by the opponent. You can use the same technique as we used for looking for splits for ourselves. That would mean that in move four in the previous Figure the JAL program needs to place a zero on position 0 (instead of 8).

12 Appendix

12.1 Programmer (Wisp628 or Wisp648)

Once you have written a program it needs to be transferred into the microcontroller. This is the task of a programmer. Some programmers can program a microcontroller while it is still in the circuit on the breadboard. This is called "in-circuit programming". Trust me, you really, really, REALLY want this feature. It gets annoying very quickly when you have to wriggle the microcontroller off the breadboard each time you forgot a comma in your program.

We'll be using the Wisp, an intelligent programmer than can handle a wide range of different PIC microcontrollers. The Wisp comes in two models, the 628 and the 648, and both can be used for the projects in this book.

feature	Wisp628	Wisp648
dongle (see 12.3)	external	built in
power supply (see 12.4)	external	built in
firmware upgradable	yes	yes
pass-though	yes	yes

Note that the Wisp648 supports more different types of microcontrollers, but none of those are used in this book.

The intelligence of this programmer is, by the way, contained in its own microcontroller; so you can make your own updated version of the programmer software if needed. Updates are available for free from the manufacturer website.

Figure 136. The Wisp628 programmer.

Also important is that this programmer has a pass-through feature. Without touching as much as a single wire you can communicate directly with the microcontroller from your

PC. This makes it ideal for debugging your software while it is running, and for interfacing.

In several projects in this book the Wisp is used in the pass-though mode. That means it is the interface between microcontroller and PC. For the 16F877(A) microcontroller these are the connections required for programming (and they can be used for pass-though too):

color	pin number	function in pass-through mode
yellow	pin 1	reset
blue	pin 40	serial out
green	pin 39	serial in
white	pin 36	
red	+5 volt	
black	0 (ground)	

If you use the Wisp648 to power your project the black and red wires are required in pass-through mode also, otherwise your project will not have any power. The Visual Basic programs in the download package are capable of switching the programmer automatically into pass-through mode[155]. The Wisp628 checkbox needs to be checked (this also works for the Wisp648)

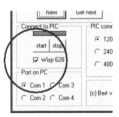

Figure 137. Checkmark for the Wisp pass-through mode.

The communication between microcontroller and PC uses pins 39 and 40, so no wires need to be changed. Because these pins do not have serial communication capabilities (the USART is connected to c6 and c7) a special library is used (software_serial). This library is part of the download package, you don't need to do anything to be able to use the pass-through mode.

---

[155] Free download from the support website http://www.boekinfo.tk (notice the way boek is spelled!)

Should you use another programmer then you need to follow the instructions that came with it. If this programmer has no pass-through mode you need to remove the checkmark and read the next section.

12.2   RS232 microcontroller - PC connection

If you use the Wisp programmer you can use the pass-through mode to make an RS232 connection between the PC and the microcontroller. The required hardware is built into the programmer, you don't need anything else, and you can skip this chapter!

If you don't use the Wisp programmer you need to build your own RS232 hardware. It is not possible to generate a true RS232 signal with a microcontroller. According to the protocol, a "0" is represented by a signal between +3 and +12 V, and a "1" by a signal between -3 and -12 V. Negative voltages are, of course, impossible for a microcontroller.

In reality, many (but not all) PCs have a rather relaxed implementation of this protocol. On the Internet you will find many schematics that use just a few simple parts to create the connection between microcontroller and PC. Apart from their low price and simplicity all have one thing in common: they work on some PCs, but not on others.

We won't bother ourselves with this and instead opt for a robust solution that works according to the official protocol. And it only costs just a few dollars in parts.

The chip we will use is the MAX202E by Dallas Semiconductors.[156] This is the pin layout:

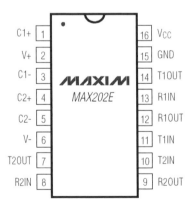

Figure 138. Pin layout of the MAX202.

---

[156]More information and the datasheet of this chip can be found on their website, http://www.maxim-ic.com.

The function of these pins is as follows:

Pin	Description
1 through 6	Connections for capacitors
7, 14	RS232 output
8,13	RS232 input
9,12	Output to PIC
10,11	Input from PIC
15	Ground (0 V)
16	Vdd (+5 V)

This gives you the ability to set up two RS232 connections with just one MAX202. In total five capacitors are needed to generate the -10 and +10 V for the signals.

In some applications the signal is inverted, which means the "0" and "1" are switched. The MAX202 uses such an inverted signal, but the Wisp programmer doesn't. If you want to use the MAX202 instead of the Wisp pass-through you'll need to make a modification to the 16F877_bert library. The best way to do it is to follow these steps:

1. Copy the 16F877_bert.jal library or the 16F877A_bert.jal library (depending on the microcontroller that you use) from the library directory [157] on your hard disk to the directory where you keep the files that belong to this project, such as the JAL source[158].
2. Start JALedit and open the library (File – Open…).
3. Search for the command *const Serial_sw_invert = false*. Change the word *false* to *true*, so that the command looks like this: *const Serial_sw_invert = true*.
4. Save the file (Ctrl-S).

When the JAL compiler searches for included libraries it first checks the directory containing the JAL program. Here it would find the modified library. If the library is not found it then checks the library directory. A library that is stored with the JAL program is called the "local copy". You can change these local copies to your liking and it won't have any effect on the other programs on your computer (because the library in the library directory is not changed).

---

[157] If you have installed the software package according to the instructions your library directory is c:\picdev\jal\libraries.
[158] This is the directory where you store your microcontroller program.

You can now transfer RS232 data with any communications package on the PC, because you don't need to use the pass-through mode. If you use MICterm you can remove the checkmark for "W*isp 628*".

To demonstrate that the hardware works this program is used to send the position of a variable resistor to the PC:

```
-- JAL 2.3
include 16F877_bert

-- define variables
var byte resist

-- define the pins
pin_a0_direction = input

forever loop

    -- convert analog on a0 to digital
    resist = ADC_read_low_res(0)

    -- send resistance to PC
    serial_sw_write(resist)
    delay_100ms(1)

end loop
```

Remember to make the changes to the library as discussed previously.

The value of the capacitors for the MAX202E is not critical. The manufacturer recommends a minimum of 0.1 uF and a maximum of 10 uF. The capacitor across the power supply pins should be at least the same capacity as the other four. This is to take care of noise on the power line, which could interfere with the proper operation of the microcontroller.[159] In this project 1 uF capacitors rated at 25 V are used. The positive and negative leads of the capacitors on pins 2 and 6 are displayed correctly in the schematic; they have to be mounted in reverse.

---

[159] The MAX202E has to increase the voltage from 5 volts to 10 volts. The mechanism used to do this, a charge pump, can easily cause nasty spikes on the power line. The capacitor prevents this. If you build this project on a circuit board don't forget the small capacitors in the power line close to the microcontroller.

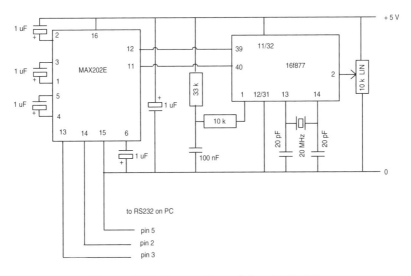

Figure 139. Connection of the MAX202.

On the PC side you only need to connect three wires. The numbers in the schematic refer to the pins on the (female) plug that you need to use. You will find these numbers on the inside of the plug. After programming disconnect your programmer and then connect the MAX202.

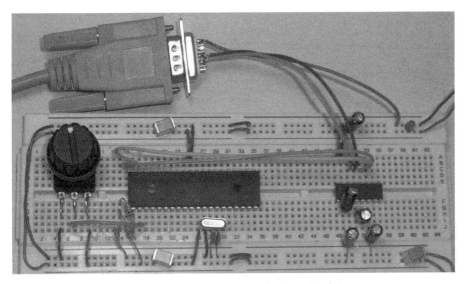

Figure 140. MAX202 (right hand side).

If you need the MAX202 often (for example because you don't have a Wisp programmer) I would recommend you build this on a circuit board. Building it on the breadboard every time you need it can get boring real quick.

12.3   Programmer dongle

This section is relevant if you own the Wisp628. If you own a Wisp648 or another programmer you can skip this section.

For some microcontrollers the pin that is used to switch the microcontroller to programming mode can also be used for other purposes. If that is the case, the power must be brought to ground during the switchover to programming mode. This is the case with the tiny 12F675. In these situations the Wisp628 needs a special dongle. For the 16F877(A) the dongle is <u>not needed</u>.

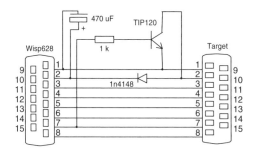

Figure 141 Dongle schematic.

Figure 142. Built dongle.

12.4 Power supply

The microcontroller used in this book use 5 volts, and that has to be rather accurate, especially during programming. Make sure to use a good stabilized power supply with a UA7805 (or similar[160]) active stabilizer, connected according to the schematic below.

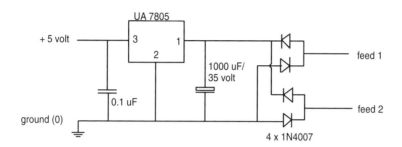

Figure 143. Stabilized 5V power supply.

A transformer is connected to feed 1 and feed 2. This may very well be a wallwart power supply, as long as the voltage is high enough. Preferably 9 to 24 volts if the transformer is alternating current (AC), or 9 to 32 volts if the transformer is direct current (DC).

It doesn't make any difference how you connect a DC transformer, since the current is still rectified by the four diodes. Of course the transformer needs to have sufficient capacity.

How much "sufficient" is depends on your project. Several hundred milliamps is usually enough. If you use more power it is advisable to equip the UA7805 with a heat sink to provide cooling[161].

Note that the Wisp648 has a built in power supply, so you only need a separate one if you use your project without the Wisp648 connected to it.

12.5 Building the robot

For several of the projects in this book you need a robot. There arc very few requirements so it should be relatively easy to built one.

---

[160] For example the LM7805 manufactured by Fairchild Semiconductor. This power regulator can handle 1 Amp max, while the UA7805 manufactured by Texas Instruments can handle 1.5 Amp.
[161] The UA7805 can deliver 1.5 Amp but that requires quite a large heat sink. For the projects in this book 1 inch^2 is more than enough, even for the robots.

The main requirements are:

1. Round.
2. Center of rotation in the center of the robot.
3. Two motors for propulsion.
4. Stabilized 5 volt power supply for the electronics.
5. Sufficient room for sensors.

If you happen to own a robot that fits these requirements you can probably use it. Most toy robots do not fit requirements one and two. That means they are less suitable for the projects in this book. For a human controlled robot the shape is not so important. Should the robot get stuck in a corner then your brain is large enough to figure out how to get it of its predicament, and if all else fails you just pick it up and put it down somewhere else.

The robots in this book are equipped with artificial intelligence of some form. If they get stuck their understanding of the world may not be extensive enough to understand how they need to maneuver to get unstuck. By making the robot round, and placing the center of rotation in the exact center of the robot it can turn within it own circumference. So if it gets stuck in a corner it can free itself by simply turning. For that reason most scientific and commercial[162] intelligent robots that need to function independently[163] are almost always round.

The base of our robot is an 11 inch grey metal pizza backing plate. By using the plate upside down (with the bend edge facing down) the sensors have free reign. The base could be a bit smaller (do make sure the breadboards, battery pack and sensors fit) but not larger, otherwise the sensor field of vision is too narrow to cover the full width.

For propulsion two 9 volt Lego[164] motors type 71427 are used. You can use any type of motor you like as long as they run slow and are strong enough to move the robot. A very low power consumption is of course an advantage. I always use Lego motors because I happen to have a bunch of them, and it makes constructing the powertrain very easy. Before you mount the motors make sure to drill a hole in the center of the plate for the wires leading to the motors. Make the hole large enough for additional wires for sensors mounted underneath the plate.

---

[162] For example the Roomba and Kärcher Roboclean vacuum clean robots, and the Scooba floor mop robot.

[163] The AIBO is not round because it doesn't have to operate independently. It is designed to play with humans and is thus under constant supervision.

[164] Technical data: max 360 rpm, 3.5 mA power consumption without load, 360 mA stalled consumption and 6 NCm stalled torque according to measurements performed by Philippe (Philo) Hurbain: www.philohome.com

For the "Breeding a robot" and "Ricochet Robot" projects you will need to mount a sensor directly above the center of rotation of the robot. It is best to leave sufficient room for that by not mounting the backs of the motors against each other.

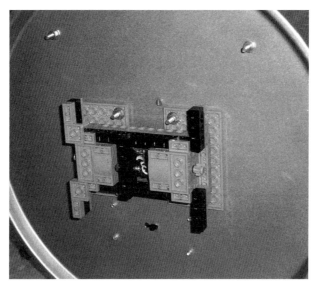

Figure 144. The two motors.

Every motor is equipped with a caterpillar track. The track is long enough to keep the robot steady even when crossing thresholds or driving over small obstacles. The disadvantage is that tracks tend to use a lot of power, so this is only suitable for strong motors. The caterpillar tracks each have three support wheels, two of which are powered.

If you use Lego motors glue the small gear to the axle otherwise it will come loose repeatedly.

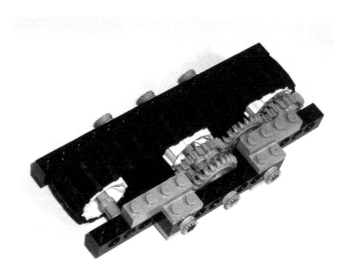

Figure 145. The caterpillar tracks powered middle and front.

If you use wheels you need to mount them in such a way that the center of rotation is exactly in the center of the robot. It is probably best to mount the wheels close to the edge of the robot for stability, and add a caster wheel for balance.

Figure 146. The power supply.

A battery pack is mounted on top of the robot at the rear. Due to the weight of the batteries the pack must be mounted over the tracks. If you use wheels and a caster wheel then the batteries should be located between them and as close to the edge as the sensors allow to maintain balance. As batteries rechargeable AA NiMH are used with a capacity of 2100 mAh. The most complicated robot in this book, the Hunter, could in theory function over 8 hours with these batteries. The batteries must be connected in series so together they generate 9 volts.

You also need to mount some brackets for the sensors. You need three in the front and one in the rear. I have used small Lego plates so the sensors can easily be placed and removed, but a metal bracket with nuts and bolts is just as good.

Near the batteries a small circuit board is used for motor control and the 5 volt stabilizer circuit. Since you need this for every robot it would be a waste of time to built this on the breadboard. In all projects it is assumed that you have built this circuit. The connections in the robot schematics refer to the connections in this circuit.

Do remember to insulate the backside of the circuit board. The robot plate is metal, so it is easy to get a short circuit.

For motor control TC4427 mosfet motordrivers[165] are used with the following specifications:

Item	Specification
peak current	1.5 A
voltage	4.5 - 18 volt
delay	30 ns
reverse current	max 500 mA

`This is more than sufficient for our application. For the power supply an UA7805 stabilizer is used, which can supply 1.5 Amp when equipped with a heat sink. A heat sink is not required for our robot, but if you plan to use it for extended periods of time it is probably better to use one. A U shaped heat sink of about 1 inch^2 is enough, alternatively you can screw the UA7805 to the base plate of the robot, which is a huge heat sink by itself.

It is probably a good idea to mount a switch on the battery pack to disconnect the power. I simply pull the connector off the pack, but a switch is much more convenient.

---

[165] PIC Microcontrollers, 50 projects for beginners and experts, Elektor ISBN 978-0-905705-70-5, page 119 - 124

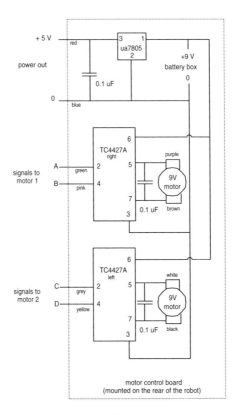

Figure 147. The robot circuit.

In order to have sufficient room for the hardware two coupled breadboards are used. The supply rail is connected to the 5 volt power supply of the robot circuit. A few decoupling capacitors of 0.1 uF are mounted on each rail to prevent oscillations.

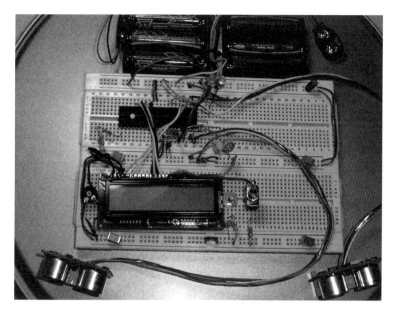

Figure 148. The breadboards are mounted and in use.

The next Figure shows the robot in operation. In this picture two of the sensor holders in front carry an ultrasonic sensor.

Figure 149. The robot taking a stroll outside.

12.6   Dual differential drive

A robot with a separate motor on each side will never run in a straight line, not even on a perfectly flat floor. Tiny differences in the motors themselves, or in the friction between gears cause an ever so slight difference in rotational speed. Apart from electronic solutions to this problem, which measure rotational speed and adjust the power to the motors, there is also a purely mechanical solution, the "dual differential drive".

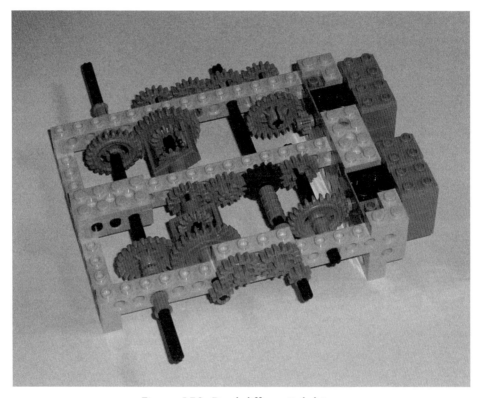

Figure 150. Dual differential drive.

This drive uses two motors; one takes care of propulsion, and one takes care of turning. Both robot wheels are powered through a differential that is mounted "the wrong way around". Normally the "casing" would be the power input, but in this system it is the power output, and thus connected to the wheels. The two power outputs of the differential are now used as inputs. One motor drives one of the inputs of both differentials in the same direction, while the other motor drives the other input of both differentials in a different direction.

So in principle both motors do not run at the same time. The center of rotation is right in the middle of the wheels. So the unit should be mounted to the robot frame in such a way that this point is exactly at the center of the robot.

The Figures show how you could build a dual differential drive. This particular configuration is based on a design by Ferrari[166]. Please note that both wheels have their own axle. The "long axle" at the back actually consists of two parts, which do <u>not</u> connect in the block in the middle.

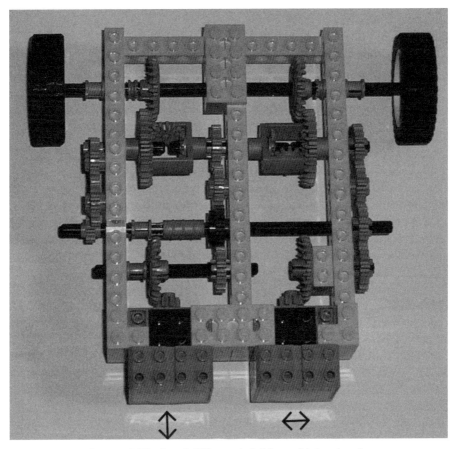

Figure 151. Dual differential drive which wheels.

The advantage of the dual differential drive is that it allows the robot to move in a perfectly straight line without the need for electronics (which require processor capacity).

[166] M. Ferrari, G. Ferrari, R. Hempel, Building Robots with Lego Mindstorm, Syngress, 2002, ISBN 1-928994-67-9, page 445-446.

The disadvantage is that quite a bit of power is lost in the gear train, and that the propulsion is now handled by just one motor. So the propulsion motor needs to be relatively powerful. If you want to use this wonderful technique you need to modify all JAL programs because they assume the more traditional setup with one motor per side.

12.7   JAL overview

In this section you will find a concise overview of the microcontroller programming language JAL and some functions from the expansion libraries. With this information you can understand the programs used in this book and adapt them to your own needs. All JAL commands and library commands that were not used in this book are not discussed, so in reality JAL and the libraries are much more powerful. If you want to know more about this great language I recommend my PIC microcontroller book[167]. This book contains a series of fun projects with detailed explanation and an extensive JAL overview. Apart form a projects book it is therefor also a JAL and microcontroller study book as well as a reference guide.

JAL[168] (Just Another Language) is a free-format language for programming PIC microcontrollers. The commands can be spread out over the lines as you please. Tabs, spaces, and newlines are all considered whitespace. There is no delimiter between different commands. In theory you could put all commands on one long line. In practice, however, appropriate whitespace results in easier-to-read programs because any convention you choose is possible. JAL is the only advanced free language, and has a large and active international user base. It is configurable and extensible by use of libraries and can even be combined with assembler.

A typical JAL program will start with a call to a library that contains relevant details for the microcontroller for which the program is written.

     include 16F877_bert

Then the variables will be declared:

     var byte a

---

[167] PIC Microcontrollers, 50 projects for beginners and experts, Elektor ISBN 978-0-905705-70-5

[168] JAL was originally designed by Wouter van Ooijen as a free high-level language comparable to Pascal. After a few years JAL continued its life as an open-source program. Since 2006 Kyle York is the chief programmer and an international user group on Yahoo can provide support.

Next are the commands:

```
forever loop
    a = a + 1
end loop
```

It is a good practice to add comments to your program to indicate what it does and for which JAL version it is written. Comment lines are preceded by two dashes or a semi colon, and ignored by the JAL compiler. A simple program might look like this:

```
-- JAL 2.3
include 16F877_bert

var byte a

-- demo program
forever loop
    a = a + 1
end loop
```

Variables

Here the power of JAL is immediately clear. Both unsigned (positive) as well as signed (positive and negative) variables can be used, containing up to 32 bits.

bit	1 bit unsigned boolean value (0 of 1)
byte	8 bit unsigned value (0 t/m255).
sbyte	8 bit signed value (-128 t/m127).
word	16 bit unsigned value (0 t/m 65,535).
sword	16 bit signed value (-32,768 t/m 32,767).
dword	32 bit unsigned value (0 t/m 4,294,967,296).
sdword	32 bit signed value (-2,147,483,648 t/m 2,147,483,647).

You can even define variables with any bit length you want, such as:

```
var bit*2 demo
```

Variable *demo* is now 2 bits long (and can thus contain the values 0, 1, 2 or 3). When a value is assigned to *demo* it doesn't necessarily have to be two bits, but only the lowest two bits will be put into the variable (the others do not fit).[169] So the statement:

demo = 99

will result in a value of 3 for *demo*, because the number 99 in binary is 1100011, and the lowest two bits are set to 1, which equals 3 in decimal.

You might perhaps expect the following calculation to allow an answer over 255, after all A is defined as a word and can be up to 65,535 large.

var word A
var byte B,C

A = B * C

In reality that doesn't happen. The compiler will multiply B and C, but since these are both bytes the result will also be a byte, and thus never larger than 255. Then the compiler will place the result in A. There would be plenty of room in A for larger numbers but by then anything over 255 is already lost. The solution is to force the compiler to use word variables while doing the calculation, like this:

var word A
var byte B,C

A = word(B) * word(C)

Besides decimal values you can use other number bases as well. In that case you need to add a prefix to the number. Possible bases are:

23   decimal (no prefix required)
0x1F   hexadecimal
0q07   octal
0b01   binary

---

[169] The compiler will notice and give you a warning. If you did it intentionally, you can ignore the warning. If you use the settings in the download package you will not see the warnings, because they are switched off by default.

And of course you can use letters:

"Hello"   string

For readability purposes underscores can be added to numbers in any position you want. To the compiler the number 10_0 is identical to 100. Binary value assignments almost always use underscores to make them easier to read:

a = 0b_1001_1110

Declaring variables must be done before they can be used. Here are a few possibilities to do this:

var byte a   *a* is declared as a byte

var byte a is b   *a* is a synonym or alias for *b* (*b* must be declared first)

The second declaration can be used to give pins names that are easier to remember. Lets suppose that a red LED is connected to pin c1. If you use this command you can refer to pin c1 using the *redLED* alias:

var bit redLED is pin_c1

For example, *redLED* = *1* would make pin c1 high and thus turn on the LED. This will make the program easier to read. But it is also easier if you want to migrate your program to another microcontroller. If this microcontroller doesn't have a pin c1, for example a 12F675 which only has port a, all you have to do is change the declaration to a pin that the microcontroller does have, such as:

var bit redLED is pin_a1

The rest of the program can then remain unchanged.

Constants

When you know in advance that a variable will be assigned a value once and will never change it is not a variable but a constant. This can be declared using *const*, like this:

const byte demo = 5

The advantage of using constants, is that a variable uses RAM memory and a constant doesn't (the compiler uses the value rather than the constant name). So it is a good idea to use constants whenever you can to save on RAM memory.

Forever loop

This command ensures that a particular part of the program is executed forever. Many microcontroller programs use this command since it is a convenient way to make sure the program never stops.

```
forever loop
      [ commands ]
end loop
```

While loop

The *while* loop executes a series of commands as long as a certain condition is met. This loop for example is executed as long as *a* is smaller than *b*:

```
while a < b loop
      [ commands ]
end loop
```

For loop

The *for* loop executes a series of commands a fixed number of times. This loop for example is executed ten times:

```
for 10 loop
      [ commands ]
end loop
```

Normally the compiler will count "internally", but you can force it to use a certain variable to count the loops, with the *using* command. This is very convenient if you want to know inside your loop how many times it has already been executed. For example, when you want to determine the position in an array. Note that *counter* will count from 0 to 9 in this program:

```
for 10 using counter loop
      [ commands ]
            value = demo(counter)
end loop
```

Procedure

A procedure is a part of program that is needed more than once. Rather than typing it several times it is put aside and given a name. This particular part of the program is only executed when it is "called" by that name. Using procedures usually makes a program easier to read and maintain.

This is an example procedure *demo*

procedure demo is
       [commands]
    end procedure

You can call this procedure simply by using the name as a command. For the procedure shown above the call would be

    demo

In procedures you can use variables just as in any other part of the program. Any variable declared outside the procedure is also valid inside a procedure. If you define a variable inside a procedure you can only use it inside that particular procedure. This is called a "local variable". For example:

    procedure demo is
        var byte a
        [commands]
    end procedure

In this example variable *a* is unknown outside the procedure.

If you want to give a value to a local variable from outside the procedure you need to "pass" it to the procedure. That particular local variable will then be declared automatically. This procedure for example declares x as a local variable of byte format:

    procedure demo (byte in x) is
        [commands that use variable x]
    end procedure

A call to this procedure would be like this, where the local variable x gets value 6:

    demo (6)

In this same way you can pass variables out of the procedure, but then you need to declare them as "*byte out*" instead of "*byte in*" in the procedure name.

This is a good way to make new commands that you can add to JAL. If you have made new procedures, for example to control a certain component or function, you can put them in a separate file. This file is then called a library and you can use it by "including" it in your program using the *include* command.

The advantage is that your program becomes much easier to read, and the next time you need that particular component or function you can simply load your library, and off you go.

Function

A function is basically the same as a procedure. The main difference is that a function always returns a value. The returned value needs to be declared using the *return* statement. In this function variable *a* is incremented by one:

```
function demo (byte in a) return byte is
    var byte b
    b = a + 1
    return b
end function
```

In the declaration of the function it is indicated that an input is expected (*byte in*) and that the answer the function will return is a byte (*return byte*). Inside the function the "*return b*" statement indicates that *b* will be the value that is returned.

This is an example of a function call:

```
x = demo(4)
```

where x will get the value 5, because $4 + 1 = 5$.

Functions are often used to return a status rather than a number, such as *true* or *false*.

If then else

This command is used to make a choice between two possibilities. *If* one condition occurs *then* something is done, *else* something else is done.

In this example *b* gets the value of 2 when *a* is equal to 1. In all other cases *b* gets 3.

```
if a == 1 then
    b = 2
else
    b = 3
end if
```

This command can be nested, like in this example.

```
if a == 1 then
    b = 2
else if a == 2 then
        b = 3
    else
        b = 4
    end if
end if
```

Note that *else if* are two words.[170] The above program yields the following results:

if	then
a = 1	b = 2
a = 2	b = 3
a = something else	b = 4

Array

Normally speaking a variable has only one value. With an array a variable can be given a whole range of variables. In the following example the *demo* array is assigned a row of five values.

    var byte demo[5] = {11,12,13,14,15}

To get a value out of the array the number between square brackets indicates the position that you want. Remember that computers start counting at 0, so the first position in the array is 0. In our example *demo[0]* contains the value 11.

This command selects the fourth number in the array (the value 14):

    a = demo[3]

---

[170] The statement *elsif* is also legal, but it is not used very often.

Adding a value to an array (or modifying one) is done in a similar way. In this command the fourth position in the array is assigned the value in *a*:

>   demo[3]= a

Your program can use the *count* statement to determine the length of an array. For example:

>   a = count(demo)

Be careful with your array size, since an array has to fit within a single RAM memory bank.

Operators

JAL has a wide variety of operators. The most important ones are shown below:

Operator	Explanation
! !	Logical. Indicates whether a variable is zero or not. For example !!5 = 1, and !!0 = 0
!	Not, or Complement. Flips 0 to 1 and 1 to 0 at the bit level. So !5 = 250 because !0b_0000_0101 = 0b_1111_1010
*	Multiply.
/	Divide without remainder. So 9/2 = 4
%	The remainder of the division So 9%2 = 1
+	Add.
-	Subtract.
<<	Left shift. Move all bits to the left by one. Note that the newly created bit is set to 0.
>>	Right shift. Same as left shift, but in the other direction. When a signed variable is shifted the sign is retained.
<	Less than.

Operator	Explanation
< =	Less than or equal to.
= =	Equal to. Note that these are two equal signs in a row. Accidentally using only one is a very common mistake (feel free to view this as an understatement)
! =	Not equal to.
> =	Greater than or equal to.
>	Greater than.
&	AND comparison at the bit level. The truth table is: 1 & 1 = 1 1 & 0 = 0 0 & 1 = 0 0 & 0 = 0
|	OR comparison at the bit level. The truth table is: 1 | 1 = 1 1 | 0 = 1 0 | 1 = 1 0 | 0 = 0
^	XOR (eXclusive OR) comparison at the bit level. The truth table is: 1 ^ 1 = 0 1 ^ 0 = 1 0 ^ 1 = 1 0 ^ 0 = 0

Comments

Lines containing comments are preceded by two dashes or a semicolon. You need to do this for each line, as there is no block comment statement.

```
; this is a comment
-- and this too
```

Comment lines are used to clarify what a program is for, or why things are done the way they are done. This is very handy for future reference, or when you want to share programs over the Internet.

It is good practice to indicate the JAL version on the very first line of your program. That eliminates a lot of questions!

Good comments are not about what a certain statement does (unless you are writing a book), because the reader may be expected to know this. They are about <u>why</u> you use the statement. If you make a library you should use comment lines to explain in detail what the library is for and how it should be used. Libraries without these comments are completely useless.

Library 16f877_bert

With the free download that comes with this book you will find a series of libraries[171] that have been combined into one big library[172] the 16F877_bert library or the 16F777A library, depending on whether you use a 16F877 or a 16F877A. This library is very popular on the Internet, because it adds a wide range of extra commands to JAL. The credit for the individual libraries within this pack goes to the individual writers.[173] Here too we only describe the commands that are used in this book, in reality the library is much more powerful.

Serial communication

The 16F887 is equipped with a serial port which can be controlled with the following commands:

serial_hw_read(data)	Receive serial data and store it in the variable *data*.
serial_hw_write(data)	Send the contents of the variable *data*.

Using software a serial connection can also be made. This is the technique used for the pass-through function of the Wisp, because it is not connected to the normal (hardware) serial port.

---

[171] Such as: 16F877_inc_all, pic_general, format, delay_any_mc, adc_hardware, pic_data_eeprom, pic_program_eeprom, pwm_hardware, serial_hardware, random, jascii, extradelay.
[172] The download package also contains standard libraries for the PICs discussed in Chapter 13: the 12F675, 16f628, and 16F876A.
[173] Stef Mientki, Wouter van Ooijen and Bert van Dam.

serial_sw_read(data)	Receive data and put it in the variable *data*.
serial_sw_write (data)	Send the contents of the variable *data*.

Contrary to hardware serial communication, software serial communication does not have a buffer. If a signal is received at the moment that the microcontroller is not actually waiting for it, it will be lost.

A/D conversion

This book only uses two commands from this extensive library:

ADC_off	Switch A/D off (all pins become digital).
ADC_read (ADC_chan)	Read the analog value on a channel into a word (channel is the AN number in the table).

Random numbers

This book only uses one command from this library:

number = random_byte	Generate a random number in the range 0 to 255.

EEPROM memory

Just two functions of this library are used.

data_eeprom_write(address,data)	Write the value in *data* to the *address* memory location in EEPROM.
data_eeprom_read(address,data)	Read the *address* memory location in EEPROM and put the contents into the *data* variable.

Other libraries

In this section libraries are discussed that are part of the download package, and are used in this book. You can use these libraries in your own programs with the *include* command. You'll also need the 16F877_bert standard library. If, for example, you want to use the lcd_44780 library your program would start with the following lines:

        include 16f877_bert
        include lcd_44780

LCD display

Commands used from the lcd_44780 library:

LCD_clear_line (line)	Clear line (note: the first line is number 0).
LCD_char_line_pos (character, line, position)	Print a character on the position and line indicated.
LCD_num_line_pos (byte, line, position)	Print a number (0 to 255) at the position and line indicated.
LCD_cursor = off	Switch the cursor off (or "on").

Robot_bert library

Block	Description
B00	Do not move.
B01(x)	Move x centimeter forward
B02	Full turn around.
B03(x)	Turn x degrees to the right.
B04(x)	Turn x degrees to the left.
B05(x)	Go x centimeter towards a light spot.
B06(x)	Go x centimeter towards a dark spot.
B07(x)	Move x centimeter backward.

12.8 Simulation in Visual Basic

Simulation

In some places in this book you will find programs that are simulated in Visual Basic before being converted to JAL and the microcontroller

If programs get very complicated the debugging possibilities of the microcontroller are somewhat limited. It is true that it is extremely simple to send data to the PC for analyses using the pass-through mode of the Wisp. But if this concerns a lot of data it can be difficult to get an overview. One could write a special program to collect and display the data, as we have done for example for the Artist and Musician programs. Sometimes however it is easier to design the program initially in Visual Basic[174], and convert it later.

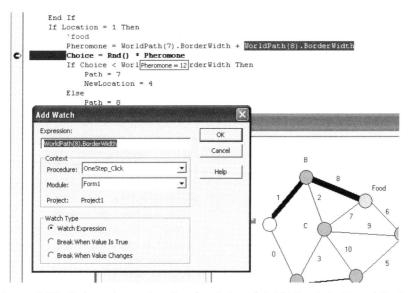

Figure 152. Debugging using Breakpoint and Add Watch in Visual Basic.

Using a few simple "debug.print" statements you can print bulk quantities of data to the PC screen to evaluate the variables. You can also use "break" the stop the program at a certain location and examine the content of variables at that spot. Or you can use Add Watch to stop the program when a variable changes. Especially when you are dealing

---

[174] Microsoft often has great actions where you can get certain versions of Visual Basic for free. Of course you can use any other programming language you fancy. Free programming software can be found at www.thefreecountry.com. Buying used software is also a good option.

with artificial intelligence programs tend to get a bit complicated, and this is very convenient development methodology.

Conversion

The similarity between Visual Basic and JAL is striking, so conversion from one language to the other is quite simple. In the next table you see a Visual Basic program next to the identical program in JAL. This particular example is from the student brain in the Teacher and his student project in section 6.3. The program has just noticed that the brain does not contain the correct answer. It will now extract a solution from the brain and adapt it, or come up with a totally new solution.

It is perhaps good to know that "RandomNumber" is a JAL procedure that yields a random number from 1 to 4, and that "MemoryGet" is a procedure to get data out of the microcontrollers EEPROM memory.

Visual Basic program	JAL program

'if the correct answer is not known
If UitTabel = 0 Then
   'make a choice from the brain table
   '(90%) or make one up an
   'answer on the spot (10%)
   selectie = Rnd(1)
   If selectie > 0.9 Or FirstRun = 1 Then
      'select 4 random numbers in the
      'range 1,2,3,4
      keuze1 = Int(Rnd(1) * 4) + 1
      keuze2 = Int(Rnd(1) * 4) + 1
      keuze3 = Int(Rnd(1) * 4) + 1
      keuze4 = Int(Rnd(1) * 4) + 1
      FirstRun = 0
   Else
      'random selection from the brain
      'table using
      UitTabel = Int(Rnd(1) * 4) + 1
 	
   'get this value from the brain table
   keuze1 = memory(UitTabel, 2)
 	
   keuze2 = memory(UitTabel, 3)
 	
   keuze3 = memory(UitTabel, 4)
	-- if the correct answer is not known
	if UitTabel == 0 then
	   -- make a choice from the brain
	   -- (90%) or make up an
	   -- answer on the spot (10%)
	   selectie = random_byte
	   if selectie > 230 | FirstRun == 1 then
	      -- select 4 random numbers in the
	      -- range 1,2,3,4
	      keuze1 = RandomNumber
	      keuze2 = RandomNumber
	      keuze3 = RandomNumber
	      keuze4 = RandomNumber
	      FirstRun = 0
	   else
	      -- random selection from the brain
	      -- table using
	      UitTabel = RandomNumber
	
	   -- get this value from the brain table
	   MemoryGet(UitTabel,2)
	   keuze1 = answer
	   MemoryGet(UitTabel,3)
	   keuze2 = answer
	   MemoryGet(UitTabel,4)
	   keuze3 = answer

Visual Basic program	JAL program
keuze4 = memory(UitTabel, 5)	MemoryGet(UitTabel,5) keuze4 = answer

'make a random mutation (90% chance)
    selectie = Rnd(1)
    If selectie > 0.1 Then
        'reset UitTabel because this is now
        'is a new value
        UitTabel = 0
        s = Int(Rnd(1) * 4) + 1
 	
        If s=1 Then keuze1=Int(Rnd(1)*4)+1
        If s=2 Then keuze2=Int(Rnd(1)*4)+1
        If s=3 Then keuze3=Int(Rnd(1)*4)+1
        If s=4 Then keuze4=Int(Rnd(1)*4)+1
    End If
  End If
End If
	-- make a random mutation (90 % chance)
	    selectie = random_byte
	    if selectie < 230 then
	        -- reset UitTabel because this is now
	        -- a new solution
	        UitTabel = 0
	        NewValue = RandomNumber
	        RandomNumber
	        if answer==1 then keuze1=NewValue end if
	        if answer==2 then keuze2=NewValue end if
	        if answer==3 then keuze3=NewValue end if
	        if answer==4 then keuze4=NewValue end if
	    end if
	  end if
	end if

You see that there is very little difference between both programs, it is almost a matter of substituting commands line by line.

A few tips for the conversion

Visual Basic	JAL
AND	&
OR	|
A conditional statement uses a single equal sign (for example *if a = 6 then*).	A conditional statement uses a double equal sign (for example *if a == 6 then*).
Array uses round brackets ()	Array uses square brackets []
At a single line *if/then* statement *end if* is not required	*End if* always mandatory.
Performs calculation with integers (-32,768 tot 32,767)	Performs calculations with bytes (0 tot 255). A good alternative would be sword (-32,768 tot 32,767) but that is not supported by all libraries. In general your JAL program will remain small and fast

Visual Basic	JAL
	if you try to stick to bytes as much as possible.
For t = 0 to 19 *Next t*	*For 20 using t loop* *end loop*
Goto and *Exit For* exist	Do not exist in JAL[175]
Comment line starts with apostrophe (')	Comment line starts with two dashes (--) or semicolon (;).
Not equal to is written as <>	Not equal to is written as !=

Variables

If you do not define a variable in Visual Basic the compiler will try to guess what you mean. This is actually quite convenient because the compiler is rarely wrong. When you want to convert a program from Visual Basic to JAL however you must take care.

A = 125 / 2
A = A * 2

In the example above Visual Basic (rightly) assumes that A must be a single[176], which yields this result:

A = 125 / 2 = 62,5
A = A * 2 = 125

In JAL however most libraries work with bytes. The reason is that the microcontroller we use, the 16F877(A) is an 8 bit (which equals a byte) microcontroller. That means the programs are small and fast if you use bytes, but become larger and slower if you use anything else. But in bytes you do get a different result:

A = 125 / 2 = 62

---

[175] Exit loop is supported in JAL 2.4i and higher. Upgrade instructions to the latest version can be found at the support website www.boekinfo.tk

[176] Single-precision floating-point, -3.402823E38 to -1.401298E-45 for negative values, and 1.401298E-45 tot 3.402823E38 for positive values.

$A = A * 2 = 124$

The best thing to do is to not let Visual Basic decide, but declare your variables as integers (as close to bytes as Visual Basic can get). Use option Explicit to help you remember to declare all your variables.

JAL commands

The real simulation enthusiasts can add JAL commands as Visual Basic subroutines. For example the *delay_100ms()* command, which would look like this as a subroutine:

```
Private Sub delay_100ms(n)
    'delay routine for JAL compatibility
    Duration! = Timer + (0.1 * n)
    Do Until Timer > Duration!
        Dummy = DoEvents()
    Loop
End Sub
```

Communication

If you want to have a Visual Basic program communicate with a JAL program you can use the following technique:

Visual Basic	JAL
number = 6 mscomm1.output=chr$(number)	
	serial_sw_read(number) number = number + 1 serial_sw_write(number)

If MSComm1.InBufferCount Then
    datapresent = MSComm1.Input
    For Counter = 1 To Len(datapresent)
        number =Asc(Mid$(datapresent, Counter, 1))
    Next Counter
End If
the number is now 7	

Please do take a look at the sources in the download package. You will find the settings for MSCommand and how to switch the programmer into pass-through mode.

Index